As Luck Would Have It

As Luck Would Have It

Incredible Stories, from Lottery Wins to Lightning Strikes

Joshua Piven

Villard / New York

Library of Congress Cataloging-in-Publication Data

Piven, Joshua.
As luck would have it: incredible stories, from lottery
wins to lightning strikes / Joshua Piven.

p.   cm.
ISBN 1-4000-6055-9
1. Fortune. I. Title.
BF1778.P58 2003
123'.3—dc21   2003041155

Villard Books website address: www.villard.com

Printed in the United States of America
on acid-free paper

24689753

FIRST EDITION

Book design by Meryl Sussman Levavi / Digitext

For Christine

In short, luck's always to blame.

—Jean de La Fontaine

Contents

Introduction

As I lifted my leg up, preparing to kick the door down, I had a flashing vision of acute, nationally televised embarrassment: Wearing shoes, not sneakers, I would slip, my left leg would come out from under me, and I would land smack on my rear end.

In the middle of Rockefeller Center.

In front of hundreds of cheering people.

In front of Al Roker and Katie Couric.

In front of millions of television viewers.

And in front of the show's musical guest, Simon Lebon and the rest of Duran Duran.

I would be a laughingstock, a national joke, an idiot. Just another first-time/last-time guest on the highest-rated morning show in the world.

It would truly be my own worst-case scenario.

But as quickly as it came, the vision disappeared. My leg was steady, my kick swift and sure. The mocked-up door splintered as I broke it down with seemingly effortless skill and, of course, raw muscle. I raised my fists into the air. A roar went up from the crowd. I had done it, I had broken down a door, just as the section in my book had described.

It worked. It really worked!

Shortly after the *Today* show segment wrapped, I rushed to the Internet-connected computer in the lobby of my New York hotel. Typing furiously, I logged on to Amazon.com. As I had many times before, I quickly scanned the page for the ranking of my book.

At that instant, *The Worst-Case Scenario Survival Handbook* was ranked number one. I was the author of the best-selling book on the planet.

◉

For good or ill, everyone has his or her own luck story. Mine began not on the *Today* show in 2000 but in Philadelphia on a blustery November afternoon in 1998.

I came home to a blinking light on my answering machine. This was not especially unusual. I was a technology journalist, one of the so-called digerati, working from a home office. By 1997 I had begun to receive a constant stream of public relations calls—most from hyperfunded dot-coms trying to "get some ink." This message was from someone whose name I didn't recognize. Often, I would simply listen to the first few seconds of such messages before hitting the delete button: I liked to do my own research, and I found calls from PR "hacks" a nuisance. I rarely returned them.

For some reason, though, I listened to this message all the way through, and what I heard was the beginning of a publishing phenomenon that would make me one of the luckiest writers in the world, and would change my life—and the lives of many other people—forever.

The message and subsequent phone conversations detailed an idea for a book that Book Soup Publishing, a fledgling book packager in town, wanted to hire me to write; they had gotten my name from a mutual colleague. The book was called *The Worst-Case Scenario Survival Handbook.* It was to be a humorous "reference" guide to surviving the disasters that often turn up in popular culture: fending off a shark, wrestling an alligator, delivering a baby in a taxicab. The outline was incomplete and the format still fuzzy, and both needed some changes. But a well-known, if quirky, publisher had already agreed to publish the book based on a brief submission. Would I be interested in writing the book, which was to be published just under a year later?

Why did I say yes? It certainly wasn't the money. I was paid a relatively small sum, which, after taxes, was less than I had been earning doing freelance marketing writing for a local architect. It wasn't the sales pitch, either. The book was presented as a simple research job, one that required perhaps some decent Internet search engine skills but very little creative thinking (though fortunately this turned out not to be the case). It wasn't even the book idea itself, which I found mildly amusing at the time but which didn't strike me as a potential hit, much less an international best-seller that would spawn numerous sequels, video and board games, a prime-time television show, countless merchandising deals, and many appearances on the *Today* show.

In the end, I agreed to write the book for two simple reasons: It was something different, which in itself was a challenge, and I had the time to do it.

Was I lucky, or was I smart? Was it fate, or was it simply opportunity that provided me with the free time to take on a book project while employed, full-time, at another job? Once I started writing the *Worst-Case Scenario* series, I began to hear even more about luck; in fact it became a constant refrain. Again and again, month after month, I would talk to experts, people who had trained their entire adult lives to survive particular situations. Then, when the day of reckoning finally arrived, when they found themselves in the very positions they had prepared for, they attributed much of their survival to luck.

How could this be? Is luck such a powerful force that it can, in an instant, wipe out years of knowledge and preparation, a lifetime of experience and expertise? Or is it something that people rely upon when other explanations are not forthcoming? Can luck be controlled, or is it inherently impossible to tame? How do the actions that we take, the people whom we know, prepare us for good luck? Or for bad luck? Is there any science behind luck, any psychology, any sociology? Or is it all simply randomness and superstition, with no order to be found, no lessons to be learned? Finding the answers to these questions got me thinking about the nature of luck and, eventually, writing this book.

❀

The dictionary tells us that luck is the favorable or unfavorable occurrence of a chance event that could not have been foreseen. Of course, we don't need a dictionary to define luck for us: It is one of the critical aspects of our lives, and it plays an important role in how we make sense of things that happen to us, and to others. You don't have to be a gambler or a fortune-teller to believe in luck. Even people who consider themselves completely rational and who disdain superstition out of hand will still utter the phrase "good luck" every now and again; perhaps they figure that the recipient believes in luck, even if they don't believe in it themselves. But believe in it or not, luck is unavoidable. *Luck* is the word we use to describe life's sudden chance moments, when our generally orderly existence takes a turn toward the random.

The purpose of this book is not to define luck in some new way; the preceding definition is sufficient. And anyway, we all know what luck is. Instead, this book seeks to examine how luck works: how it affects people, how people react to it, and how we can learn about it from the experiences of others. Because the impact of luck is more often than not dependent on the personality of the lucky (or unlucky) recipient, the book also seeks to understand people's beliefs about luck: How do people understand lucky events? How does luck affect people's behavior? How do they react to good and bad luck? How do they account for it? How do people integrate life-changing lucky events into their overall understanding of what life is about? And what can we learn from their experiences? The book will, I hope, answer at least some of these questions, and perhaps get the reader thinking about some others as well.

As Luck Would Have It also tries to bring together some disparate theories about how people's actions and attitudes can affect their reactions when confronted with particularly good or bad luck. Does having a positive outlook on life make us more likely to benefit when good luck comes our way? Conversely, are we more likely to be prepared for the worst luck throws at us if we are actually negative thinkers? Can we even prepare for luck at all? How do our social and business networks—the groups of people who surround us—contribute to our lucky break, or our unlucky accident?

It is interesting that what research there is on the phenomenon of luck is quite limited in scope. While existing studies deal primarily with the psychological underpinnings of those who think they can control luck (particularly gamblers), they tend to use as their subjects paid volunteers in a lab setting.

This book tries a different approach. Rather than put people in front of a computer screen, or deal them cards from the bottom of the deck, it uses as its subjects people who have actually experienced incredible strokes of good and bad luck in their lives: lottery winners, plane crash survivors, lightning strike victims, discoverers of important scientific findings, inventors of fads, successful businesspeople, musicians, and others. Their amazing experiences serve as our window into the province of luck, and help us understand how luck works in the real world, not simply in a lab.

However, while the book is not intended to be a scientific treatise on luck, it does touch on some of the more interesting research findings in related fields, including the intriguing possibility that even an irrational belief that we can control luck can help us perform better in our daily lives. Other interesting and relevant topics are also included, such as the power of anxiety to manage luck, the connections between luck and religion, and the ways that the people we know, even slightly, can have disproportionate impacts on our luck. At the same time, the book acknowledges that luck does not occur in a vacuum. Timing and luck are closely related, and for this reason the book examines many social, cultural, political, and even meteorological events that help to explain why some people get lucky and others do not.

❀

Some years ago, an article in *Life* magazine told an almost unbelievable tale of incredible luck.

On a cool March night, it seems that all fifteen members of a church choir in Beatrice, Nebraska, were late for practice, scheduled to begin at their church at 7:20 in the evening. The members had different reasons for their tardiness: two were waiting to hear the end of a radio program, two others had car trouble, another was trying to finish a math problem, one took a while to wake up from a nap, and so on.

At precisely 7:25 P.M., the church was destroyed by an explosion. The members of the church, the *Life* writer reported, wondered if the fortuitous delays had been "an act of God."

While the choir members in this story wondered if they should attribute their survival to the hand of God, many of us simply use the word *luck* to describe such chance events, good or ill, that affect our lives. The desire to find explanations for random events is constant, and universal: As *Homo sapiens,* we seek to understand, to determine meaning, and to impose order on events, chance or not.

While such events may be monumental (winning the lottery) or relatively ordinary (arriving at the station just as the train pulls in), they nevertheless illustrate that chance is an important and unavoidable part of life. And, critically, even chance events that seem to be minor when they occur can have causal effects far out of proportion to their initial importance. Consider the following lines:

For want of a nail, the shoe was lost;
For want of a shoe, the horse was lost;

> For want of a horse, the rider was lost;
> For want of a rider, the battle was lost;
> For want of a battle, the kingdom was lost!

The verse nicely illustrates what is sometimes called the "butterfly effect," technically known as *sensitive dependence on initial conditions.* (The nickname comes from the idea that even the tiny changes in air currents created by a butterfly flapping its wings create a series of magnified results that eventually can change the weather across the globe.) The butterfly effect is central to chaos theory and also applies to chance events like good or bad luck, which from a seemingly minor starting point can alter our lives forever in an instant.

Thus, for better or worse, an instance of luck is both inevitable and a powerful force of change in our lives. The stories of luck in these pages are all true, and the people who experienced them are real (a few names have been changed to protect privacy). Each of their lives has been shaped, in many ways, by a singular, split-second event that occurred by chance, and over which they had no control. Like the proverbial butterfly flapping its wings, from that blink of an eye lives followed uncharted and unpredictable courses, courses determined by luck.

Some of the people described in the book are still dealing with the repercussions of their luck, and are still learning about how the events altered their lives. Some spent years trying to come to grips with their luck, while others moved on with nary a look back. But all were affected in some way. From their experiences, and from their beliefs about them, we gain considerable insight into the ways we might manage our own luck, when it happens to come our way.

JOSHUA PIVEN, JUNE 2003

As Luck Would
Have It

CHAPTER 1

Do Not Rip the Ticket or
Otherwise Mutilate It

Steve Roberts is having trouble reading the numbers.

It's dark outside, and he's driving, so try as he might, he can barely make them out. It's late, and he's tired, and the woman on the radio is announcing the winning numbers over and over, since the drawing was hours ago, and the winning combination was sold. Yet still no one has come forward to claim the jackpot. With his ten tickets, each containing ten series of numbers, there's no way he can listen to the announcer on the radio, watch the road, and read the tickets at the same time. Instead, he tries a quick glance at each Big Money Ball number, knowing that, without that number, there's no chance he'll win the Big Game.

But it's no use, he just can't see the numbers. He doesn't bother pulling over, since it's after 11:00 P.M. and he's tired. He's had a long day putting in and inspecting pools in the Michigan suburbs, where, in May 2000, the hot, humid summer—his busy season—is just getting under way. He gives up on the tickets. And anyway that hot dog he ate at lunchtime, the one he bought just before he decided to pick up some tickets, isn't sitting too well. He'd just as soon get home, see his wife and kids, maybe have a beer and a snack, and go to bed.

What are the odds that he's the winner? Who ever heard of a guy like him winning the Big Game? Much less today's jackpot, the biggest in the history of any lottery. And anyway, he's never even bought a lottery ticket in his life. Wasn't it always the guys who bought a ticket every day for twenty years who won? He puts the tickets back into his pocket and laughs—a tired, exhausted, end-of-a-long-day laugh. Then he sighs.

What was it up to now? Something like $363 million? He pulls into his driveway. It's nearing 11:30, and he has to be up early in the morning. He sighs again.

❖

A lottery win is luck in its purest form: unexpected, unpredictable, and with external causes over which we have absolutely no control. And, of course, there are the tremendous odds. These vary with the game and the number of tickets sold, but the odds of winning a multistate lottery are in the tens or scores of millions to one. These odds generally rise in direct proportion to the dollar amount of the potential payout: More money means more media hype, which means more people buying more tickets, which means a larger jackpot, which starts the cycle all over again.

But winning a big-money lottery game, while clearly lucky, often comes with a price, and that price can quickly turn untold millions into a liability instead of an asset. With big money comes big publicity, and on the heels of publicity come those looking for an investment, a loan, or simply a handout. Furthermore, many lottery winners are unprepared for their huge tax liability and for the suddenly needy relatives, the scheming business associates, and the jealousy and resentment of their friends and colleagues. Add in the huge psychological burden of dealing with sudden wealth and you get a depressing but sobering statistic: Two out of every three lottery winners either lose or spend all their winnings within five years.

Still, winning the lottery may seem like a problem well worth having. That wouldn't be me, we think. I'd invest all my money. I'd play it safe. But the fact is that managing the good luck of a lottery win is not as easy as it might seem. Several researchers have even identified a psychological disorder, termed "sudden wealth syndrome," that can result from a large influx of money and can severely hamper our day-to-day ability to function in the world. And these symptoms can afflict those who get sudden, unexpected wealth not just from a lottery ticket but via an inheritance, or even from an unexpected business success. Examining the story of Steve Roberts can tell us much about how we can manage the good luck of sudden wealth in our lives, so that we can learn how to use good fortune to remain fortunate.

○

Roberts (he asked that his real name not be used) is a workaday guy, albeit one with a fairly successful swimming pool contracting business. At age forty-eight, he's doing pretty well for himself, bringing in $100,000 in a good year, although like everyone he knows he's also saddled with a mortgage and a car payment. With one son still in college and his daughter about to enter high school, he's having trouble keeping his savings in the five digits. Still, things are pretty good, and with a few more hot summers, he figures he might be able to dig a pool for himself.

The Big Game is a seven-state combined lottery. By May 2000 it has rolled over so many times that everyone has lost track of when the last Big Money Ball winner was. While many people pick the winning five numbers, they win only smaller payouts, generally about $150,000 each before taxes. Unless you have all five numbers and the Big Money Ball number, you do not win the jackpot. The May 2000 Big Game jackpot, at $366 million, is the largest in U.S. history, eclipsing even 1998's $296 million Powerball jackpot, which had been split among thirteen lucky Ohio machinists. (A December 1999 Spanish lottery, called El Gordo, was valued at $1.2 billion but was split among thousands of winners.)

The night before the May 9 drawing, Peg, Steve's wife, sees a news story on the size of the jackpot, now over $300 million, making the pot the most valuable in the history of multistate lotteries. Peg is by no means a gambler; she's never even dropped a nickel in a slot machine. In fact, she and Steve have good-naturedly teased their friends about buying lottery tickets. With the odds against winning so high, what's the point? You'd probably have a better chance striking oil in your backyard!

Still, she thinks, so much money! What would anyone possibly do with it all? Give it away to family and friends, she supposes, and to charity. And pay off the mortgage, of course. Pay off the car. She comments to Steve on the size of the jackpot and, with skepticism thick in his voice, he agrees that, if he's somewhere where he can pick up a ticket quickly, he will. But he knows he probably won't: He has a full day of work on Tuesday, and he's seen the news stories, too. Those lottery places have lines stretching around the block.

The next day Steve has of course forgotten all about the Big Game. Instead, he's thinking about the pools he needs to inspect and, if necessary, repair. With the weather getting hot already, he knows that by Memorial Day suburban Michiganites will be clamoring for relief from the stifling humidity.

At lunchtime, Steve heads over to Mr. K's Party Shoppe, twenty miles north of Detroit, to pick up a hot dog and a Coke. While standing at the counter, he suddenly realizes that the store has a lottery machine and, even more amazingly, there is no line at all. He opens his wallet, figuring that he'll pick up a ticket with the few loose dollars in his pocket, but quickly realizes that all he has is a hundred-dollar bill. He pays for the hot dog and, figuring what the hell, asks for his change in lottery tickets, receiving ninety-eight one-dollar tickets. He's never played before, so he doesn't have a lucky number, and anyway he's in a hurry, so he just asks the kid behind the counter for "easy picks," random numbers generated by the lottery machine. The clerk asks him if he wants the lump-sum payout or the annuity option; the annuity pays more in the long run, of course, but gives him no control over how his "winnings" are invested. He chooses the annuity. He laughs to himself. He can always change his option later, after he wins.

That night, as he fumbles with the tickets in his truck, he again wonders why he bothered buying them—and why he bought so many. He's hardly rich, and he's not a gambler (except occasionally on a game of pool). Ninety-eight dollars, while not likely to break the bank, is still a decent amount of money for him, and lottery tickets are not exactly a smart investment. Indeed, for someone like him, a strong believer in saving for the future, buying lottery tickets seems more like voodoo economics than sound financial planning. Oh well, he thinks, we all make rash decisions now and then.

As he listens to the voice on the radio, he glances down one last time. He does not see a matching Big Money Ball number, although in the darkness he can't be sure. But who knows, maybe he's just won $150,000. That wouldn't be so bad. After taxes, it comes to something near a hundred grand. He could live with that.

When he finally gets home, he's so tired he goes to bed immediately.

○

The next morning, as Peg pours orange juice, they watch the early news. The talk show *Good Morning America* is interviewing twenty-three-year-old Melvin Kassab, the man who sold the winning ticket. Steve comments to Peg that he looks really familiar. In a second he makes the connection and says to his wife, "That's the kid from Mr. K's, the one who sold me my tickets!" Peg thinks for a second, then asks Steve how closely he looked at the lottery tickets last night. Their eyes lock, and she immediately goes over to the counter and grabs the tickets, still sitting in a neat pile where her husband left them last night. She looks at the first of the ten tickets, reads the Big Money Ball number, then says quietly, "Steve, we have the Big Money Ball."

But it can't be. It must be a mistake. They both check again, carefully comparing the numbers on the ticket with the winning numbers, which are coming up on the screen every few seconds: 33, 2, 1,

12, 37, and Big Money Ball 4. They look at one another, freeze, and then time stops completely.

❉

What is it like to realize, in an instant, that you have suddenly become one of the richest people in America? Not by merit, not by hard work, not by good fortune (as in an inheritance), but rather by pure luck—indeed by virtually the purest form of luck, unplanned, unexpected, against incredible, almost unfathomable odds, and by a means that you have eschewed your entire adult life.

There's no single emotion, or rather there are too many emotions at the same time. Steve Roberts experiences a very brief period of elation, followed by a period of abject terror. What if someone realizes he has the winning ticket and tries to steal it? What if the ticket gets lost or, worse, damaged? What if someone does something to his kids, perhaps a kidnapping? He quickly calls the Michigan Lottery Commission and is asked to read the validation numbers below the bar code printed on the ticket. He does, and they confirm that he is the winner. Then come the warnings: Do not get the ticket wet, or it is null and void. Do not rip the ticket or otherwise mutilate it, or it is null and void. And please, do not lose the ticket.

For half an hour, Steve and Peg do not speak. Alone, each contemplates the unimaginable wealth they have just been handed. How much will it be? A hundred million? Two hundred million? More? And what difference would it make if it *was* more? Would they really be able to spend an extra hundred million? What if there are multiple winners? What will their take be then? How much will they give to their families? To charity? Will they move away from Michigan? Where will their daughter go to school?

Steve quickly puts the ticket in a waterproof bag. He and Peg drive to their daughter's school and make up an excuse to pull her out. Then the three of them drive to the Michigan State Lottery Commission offices, where a throng of reporters has already gathered. Because more than twenty people had picked the correct five numbers (but not the Big Money Ball), there are many other winners arriving, each entitled to a $150,000 payout. With each arrival, the shouting begins anew: "Are you the Big Game winner?" "Did you win the big money?" "How much did you win?"

Fearing for his family's safety as well as their privacy, Steve says nothing as he enters the building. After validating his ticket, the lottery commission decides on a ruse to protect the family's privacy for the time being. Steve will be issued one of the large "TV checks" that winners hold up in front of the television cameras. Except, they all agree, his check will read $150,000, not the $181.5 million that he's actually won (there was one other Big Money Ball winner). Steve is relieved, but he knows it's only a temporary reprieve. By law he will be forced to go public when the lottery commission officially announces he's won.

The commission begins to tell him the practical ramifications of his extraordinary luck. His $181.5 million? Since he's suddenly in the highest tax bracket, it's closer to $120 million, after paying the tax man. Does he want the lump sum or the twenty-year annuity? He changes his former preference and chooses the lump sum, and the payout instantly shrinks to $90 million. Does he plan to give any of his winnings away? Of course. Does he realize that gifts over $10,000 are subject to the federal gift tax? No, he hadn't known that. To avoid this tax, he is informed, Steve will need to form a "lottery club," basically a partnership that allows his designated recipients to share in his winnings without paying the tax. His head spinning, Steve must now decide who will join this exclusive club, and how much money each member will receive.

With so many decisions to make, Steve decides to go home and do some thinking. But when he pulls into their street, he sees a crew from Channel 7, the local ABC affiliate, in front of the house. Has there been a leak? Does the press know he's the big winner? Soon more news crews show up, and Steve decides he needs to get his family out of the house. After they contact a friend in the Justice Department, Steve and his family are spirited to a hotel in Frankenmuth, Michigan, for the night. There, finding sleep impossible, he begins to think about how he will distribute his winnings.

He decides to give his immediate family members—mothers, fathers, brothers, sisters—$500,000 each. He also decides to pay off the mortgages of other family members, including aunts and uncles, which will allow them to take early retirement. He will pay the college tuitions of some nieces and nephews, and buy new cars for his two grown sons. Because of estate tax laws, he also decides to set up annuities for his children. And he will give lots of money to various charities.

Next morning, the official press circus begins. Steve and his family have been driven, via limousine, to the civic center in Lansing, the state capital. There, entering through an underground garage, they take Governor Engler's private elevator to a meeting room, where they are officially congratulated by the governor. With a press agent supplied by the lottery commission at his side, Steve enters the press conference room. Packed with reporters, the press conference is nationally televised, and the questions are pretty much what he expected. "How does it feel?" "What are you going to do with the money?" "How often do you play the lottery?" It's all a blur. At some point, Steve's press agent informs him that there is a list of two hundred people seeking interviews. Invitations from the morning shows begin pouring in. Steve flies to New York to appear on the *Today* show and *Live with Regis & Kathie Lee.* He is interviewed by Bryant Gumbel and Diane Sawyer.

Then, almost as soon as it began, the publicity starts to fade. Within a week the nationals stop calling. After two weeks even the local news reporters pack up their equipment and drive off. Steve is finally able to get back to his life. He decides to work through the summer, at least to finish the jobs he began in the spring. But he soon realizes that his old life is gone. It's as if, at age forty-eight, he's been born into a new existence, one with incredible wealth but also incredible pressures, pressures that he's never experienced before. He now has a new job: wealth management. And everyone's got a hand out.

○

A recent survey by *Forbes* found that 37 percent of the four hundred richest Americans are unhappy. According to Steve, there's much truth in the old saw that money can't buy happiness. "Money can't make you happy, but it can make you more unhappy," he says. In fact, psychologists have coined a term, *affluenza,* to describe a wide range of symptoms that can result from sudden wealth, including shame, anger, fear, guilt, and rampant materialism. Affluenza, sudden wealth syndrome, or whatever the diagnosis, the condition of being instantly rich can have profound consequences, not only psychologically but also socially.

Steve discovered that his good fortune meant acquaintances and friends soon began asking for loans or "investments" in their businesses. He found that normal conversations he had had in his "pre-luck" life were now emotionally charged land mines, forcing him to filter his words. "In the past, if one of my friends got a new car, it was naturally a topic of conversation," he recalls. "But now, if I talk about a new car, it's bragging."

Similarly, Steve found it difficult to maintain some of his former hobbies, because his newfound wealth was always a topic of conversation. "I used to really enjoy playing competitive pool, and I played in some tournaments," he says. "But now, people say, 'Why is he playing? He doesn't need the money.' So I don't compete anymore. Simple things just become much more complicated." While he maintained his close friendships, other people became standoffish and, eventually, drifted away.

Indeed, psychologists have found that, while acquiring a vast sum of money can make life easier in many ways, it often makes personal relationships much more difficult. "A flood of economic power can be really destabilizing to your sense of personal balance," says Mark Levy, a California psychiatrist and assistant professor of psychiatry at the University of California, San Francisco. In particular, those who are not born into wealth but rather acquire it through luck (the lottery, the stock market) or other means (business success) often lack the skills necessary to manage money, not simply financially but in their relationships as well. Coming into money will also fundamentally test the basis of relationships, many experts say, and will quickly make bad or unhealthy relationships worse.

Steve continually encountered friends and even slight acquaintances who asked to borrow money, and he mostly obliged them. He estimates that "99 percent" of them came back for more. "At the beginning, you just have no comprehension of the power you have, the responsibility that comes with having so much wealth," he says.

❀

In addition to some relationships, Steve finds that his privacy is slowly disappearing. While the media have mostly found other fish to fry, he begins to get constant phone and mail solicitations, everyone from financial managers with risky schemes to quacks with penis enlargement "investment opportunities." Eventually he sells his house and moves into a more secluded home with an unlisted telephone number.

His vast wealth also gives him opportunities, of course, and he begins to contribute to numerous charities. Finding that with each subsequent big jackpot the media seek him out for interviews, he includes as a condition of his participation that he be allowed to mention his favorite charitable causes. And, while still fully aware of the odds, for six months after his luck event he buys one hundred tickets a week for the Big Game and gives them away to friends. Nobody wins.

He also buys some toys, including a few cars and a nice boat. He eventually builds a second home in Arizona and makes various real estate investments. He chooses an investment strategy that puts 10 percent of his money into equities, about 55 percent into tax-free municipal bonds and Treasury bills, and the rest into real estate and cash. He and Peg do volunteer work. And he plays a lot of golf.

❀

Is Steve Roberts happy? He certainly sounds happy, and in interviews he indicates that he is. He tends to be an optimist, and he says that others would generally describe him as a positive person. He is not especially religious, or even spiritual, though he believes in God. And, unlike many lottery winners, he is a deliberate and careful planner, especially when it comes to financial planning for the future.

Does being incredibly rich account for Steve's happiness? Clearly, it has made his life easier. But Steve indicates, and numerous psychological studies confirm, that money and happiness are not intrinsically related. In fact, research has shown that people's well-being does not improve as their wealth increases. Indeed, it tends to demonstrate the opposite: Namely, that the successful pursuit of materialistic goals brings little in the way of enhanced well-being. Money, it seems, can make some things easier. But it does not, on its own, make life better.

Of course, as a good-luck event in and of itself, winning the lottery—particularly a big-money jackpot—can have profound effects on one's material quality of life. In practical terms, receiving *any* windfall (an inheritance, valuable stock options) can have many of the same consequences, eliminating the worry about one's day-to-day needs. But good luck, in this case, also demands good management skills. These skills include not simply the effective management of financial issues but the care and feeding of familial, social, and societal relationships as well. Steve's experience shows that while generosity with family members can make an important difference in their lives, loaning (or giving) money to friends and acquaintances, tempting as it can be, may simply leave them wanting more.

Much may depend on the wants and perceived needs of individuals, of course, and what people do with money once they get it.

But evidence abounds that wealth and relative happiness are virtually unrelated. Recent studies have shown that the most satisfying life experiences stem from the fulfillment of the top four human psychological needs: autonomy, competence, relatedness, and self-esteem. In virtually all cases, those whose experiences meet these top four needs are happier than those whose experiences do not. Other needs, including physical thriving, security, meaning, and pleasure, rank lower in importance but are still necessary for fulfillment. Ranking at the bottom of the scale? Money, and luxury.

In order to truly make us happy, money should fulfill needs other than those based simply on material desires. We need to use the luck of "found money" to help others as well as ourselves, not just in financial terms but in creative ways that give them the freedom to achieve their own goals and to seek personal fulfillment. Perhaps, as in Steve's case, this means paying off a mortgage to allow someone to work less and enjoy her hobbies more. Perhaps it means paying for an education that was otherwise difficult or impossible to obtain. Or it may mean the donation of our time and effort to charities—which often value such gifts more than money.

In the end, it seems that hitting the jackpot means little if we cannot use our good luck to make luck for those less fortunate. This entails careful planning, generosity, and perhaps most important, an understanding that sudden wealth is a means to an end, not an end in itself.

Is Steve now a believer? As someone who had never played the lottery before—indeed, as someone who ribbed those who did—does he now advocate playing regularly? Not really. "I still know the odds," he admits. But he does acknowledge that, for many people, the lottery represents hope (albeit hope against the odds) that something better might come along, and he recognizes this is an important emotion that can't, and perhaps shouldn't, be summarily dismissed.

Is it misplaced hope? Possibly. But as Steve says, someone has to get lucky.

CHAPTER 2

Staying Put Means Giving Up

Bennet Zelner is waving frantically at the small helicopter hovering just above the tree line, but no one is waving back.

He's in a clearing, on the edge of the woods, on the side of a snow-covered mountain, screaming at the top of his lungs, waving, trying to make them see him. How come they don't do anything? Can't they hear him? Can't they see him? He's wearing an orange parka! What's wrong with them? Please, please, just let them show that they've seen him! A wave, a horn, a flare, anything! Why won't they acknowledge him?

The helicopter hovers above him for a few more seconds, then flies off, leaving Bennet in silence once again. Dejected, starving, his feet frozen, his energy gone and his hope fading, he struggles to keep from falling over. He knows the helicopter was probably his last chance. His strategy has failed. He'll never make it another night out here, and the snow is too deep to go on. Is this it? Is it possible that this is how it ends, here in the snow in the cold on a mountain?

Then he sees distant movement in the trees. A rabbit! Food! He hasn't eaten in days. Perhaps he can catch it somehow and then figure out how to cook it.

At least he'll die full.

◉

Bennet readily admits to anyone who asks that he's a city kid. Although he's done some skiing out West, he's still more at home dodging traffic than finding his way in the wilderness. After growing up in New York City, he went to Brown University, living in Providence, then lived in Los Angeles for several years before moving to Berkeley to attend U.C. Berkeley's doctoral program in business administration. At five feet six inches and slim, he's not going to be mistaken for a lumberjack. But he's certainly not a geek, either: He enjoys the outdoors and by 1995, at age twenty-six, has become an avid cyclist, sometimes riding twenty-five miles a day, much of it up and down the steep hills in and around the Berkeley campus. With his curly dark hair and striking blue eyes, he's never had a problem getting a date, and his self-effacing humor and intelligence make him a fun—and funny—guy to be around.

And yet, at Berkeley, something is missing. In his second year of grad school, his social life is somewhat lacking, and the stress of the program is getting him down. While certainly no slouch academically (he majored in public policy and economics), he's been finding it hard to concentrate on his studies, and now, during winter break, he's been procrastinating on a paper he should have started writing weeks ago. It's in this frame of mind that he gets a phone call with a ready-made excuse to put off his paper for just a few more days. His friends Greg Bashaw and Fernanda Moore, along with Greg's brother Jeff and his girlfriend, Melanie, are heading up to Lake Tahoe to stay at Greg's mother's cabin for a few days. Is Bennet interested in coming along?

The timing of the invitation couldn't be better. Bennet has decided that this is the winter he's really going to work on improving his skiing. A relatively proficient intermediate, he can handle the "blues" without a problem, and can even make it down most expert trails, albeit slowly and with the occasional wipeout. Somewhat of a risk taker ("probably the result of an overprotective mother," he later recalls), he likes a challenge, even if that means overestimating his abilities every now and then, like that time with the sailboat. What had he been thinking?

He and his friends had anchored a small boat in a cove near Treasure Island in San Francisco Bay. They had waded to shore, then walked around the edge of the cove for a picnic.

On the way back, Bennet decided to swim directly out to the boat rather than walk "the long way" to the dock, a distance of several hundred yards. About halfway out, in the freezing cold water, he realized he'd made a horrible mistake. Never a great swimmer, he'd been trying to impress his friends, and now he was exhausted. Like many novice swimmers, he had also underestimated the power of the current, and though he still had a long way to go, it was pulling him out into the bay. With supreme effort, he finally made it. An old man just stared at him as Bennet struggled up onto the dock. Waiting for the man to ask him if he was okay, Bennet was lying on the splintered wood, panting, trying to catch his breath.

"Pretty stupid," said the man.

But that was Bennet. Smart, if sometimes just a little bit stupid.

❖

On Tuesday, January 3, 1995, the group of five, relaxed and look-ing forward to a few days in the mountains, piled into the car for the four-hour drive up to Tahoe, and Alpine Meadows Ski Area. With the radio blaring, the occasional cigarette, and lots of good conversation, it was the start of a great trip. Greg and Jeff knew that their midweek arrival meant no crowds, and thus no lift lines. Perhaps they would even go for the untouched powder in the challenging back basin, the backside of the mountain, where the steep terrain, heavily wooded ravines, and limited lift service meant experts only.

As they approached Donner Summit, the rain of the lower eleva-tions turned to a white mist, then slowly to flurries, then quickly to a swarm of tiny, paperlike flakes of fine white snow.

This was the beginning.

❖

On Wednesday, his first full day of skiing, Bennet is really enjoying his new skis and boots, although he's annoyed with himself for hav-ing forgotten ski pants. Luckily he was able to borrow a pair of thin nylon cross-country-ski pants, which he wears over silk long underwear, but the waist is too big and they keep slipping down his wiry frame. And they're barely waterproof. His glasses are also con-stantly fogging up, making it difficult to see through the swirling flakes. His vision isn't really that bad, so he's taken to removing his glasses on the downhill runs, stuffing them in the pocket of his parka.

He makes a mental note to buy prescription ski goggles for next season.

The conditions are phenomenal. It's been snowing steadily, and heavily, for days, and for the first time Bennet's getting to enjoy the incomparable feeling of making "fresh tracks" in virgin snow. What a feeling, slicing through new powder, the feather-light snow flying behind him. He does, however, wish that he had someone to ski with. His friends are either highly proficient skiers or beginners, while he's somewhere in between. With little desire to meander down the relatively flat bunny trails or suffer through the expert runs, he tackles the intermediate trails by himself, and they all meet once or twice a day for a steaming cocoa by the fire in the lodge.

It's midafternoon when the group gathers in the warm lodge, each with that perfect mixture of exhilaration, exhaustion, and burning muscles unique to a great day on the slopes. After a short rest, the five agree to take a few more runs, then meet up and head back to the cabin for beers. They wish one another a good run, then separate. It is 2:45 P.M. on Wednesday, January 4.

❊

The winter of 1994–95 was one of the wettest on record in California.

Beginning in September, storm after storm barreled in from the Pacific, pounding lower elevations with unrelenting rainfall. Counties like Mendocino and Humboldt got as much as forty inches of rain, causing widespread flooding and millions of dollars in damage. In the first two weeks of January alone, Shasta Lake—at twenty thousand acres California's largest reservoir—had risen fifty feet, at one point rising six inches an hour.

High above the valleys, in the steep mountain peaks of the Sierra, the precipitation was piling up as snow, in totals unseen for generations. By Thanksgiving 1994, Mammoth Mountain, the largest ski resort in central California, was reporting a snow base depth of ninety inches; a base of a few feet was typical for November. Mammoth had opened for skiing on October 8, its earliest opening date ever. One observer likened driving up California's Interstate 80, the main highway to the Sierra, to driving through a snow tunnel: Piles of snow, some fifteen feet high, lined the road. Owners of mountain homes opened their doors to find five feet of fresh snow—on the roof. The snow was light and airy, a dream for expert skiers and "powder hounds." Some reported the best trail conditions ever, and many were skiing in snow up to their necks.

But it wasn't all fun and frolic in the Sierra that winter. In addition to their constant clearing of the roads, California State and Placer County officials were busy worrying about avalanches and lost or injured skiers. On December 4, 1994, Alan Austin, an attorney from Atherton, California, vanished while skiing during a whiteout. An experienced skier, he survived for two nights in freezing temperatures by digging a snow cave and using it for shelter from the massive storm. During one of the few breaks in the snowfall, he was sighted and plucked from the side of a mountain by a Marine Corps rescue helicopter. Austin had been skiing at Squaw Valley, directly across the KT Ridge from Alpine Meadows, the location where he was discovered on December 6.

At Squaw Valley, site of the 1960 Winter Olympics, the December storms that enveloped Alan Austin were only the opening act of a severe winter drama. A virtually unprecedented fourteen feet of snow, or nearly a foot per day, fell in the two-week period beginning January 4.

It was against this backdrop, on January 4, in the midst of a howling blizzard, that Bennet Zelner took an Alpine Meadows chairlift and became the second person that season to disappear into the wilderness.

◦

Without looking at his trail map, which is crumpled into a ball in his pocket, Bennet figures he'll try a new trail on another section of the mountain. From the top of the lift, he chooses a relatively flat, meandering trail that leads him to the top of another trail, this one running directly below a chairlift. With the snow coming down heavily and visibility just a few yards, he decides to play it safe and follow the trail below the lift, which he assumes will bring him back to the lodge. He skies down slowly, his legs beginning to feel heavy after hours on the slopes.

When he arrives at the bottom of the chairlift, Bennet is confused. There are no people about, and no sign of a building or lodge. Assuming that he's simply arrived at one of the mid-mountain lifts, he considers going back up, then skiing down in a different direction. But with the poor visibility and fading daylight, he rejects this option, instead choosing what appears to be a flat connector trail. He hopes this trail will lead back to one of the main trails, which he can then follow to the base lodge. He doesn't bother to consult the soaked trail map in his pocket. Although he has no watch, he figures from the dimming light that it's about 3:00 or 3:30 P.M. He pulls up his neck warmer and pulls down his wool hat to cover his freezing ears. He'd better hurry if he's going to meet his friends at 4:00.

For ten minutes he skis on the relatively flat trail as the storm builds and the light fades. Finally, with no lodge, chairlift, or lift tower in sight, he decides to turn around, figuring it's better to climb back up the hill than to continue skiing off into the unknown. And anyway, there are clearly no recent tracks on this trail, so for all he knows it goes to some disused lift or utility shack. He knows it's probably going to take him a while to get back up, but he's fit, and he's got a decent sense of adventure. He clicks open his bindings, steps out of his skis, and immediately sinks to his knees in the powdery fluff.

Undaunted, he begins a laborious hike back the way he came, with the snow silently piling up all around him. He's left his skis, assuming he'll return tomorrow and pick them up; they're practically brand-new, and they're his first pair. He's not about to lose them.

But he quickly realizes the folly of his decision. Sinking nearly to his waist, even to his chest in some places, he's getting winded, and he's barely made any progress. Making a snap judgment to return to his skis and try another course of action, he turns back and heads down the trail. But it's snowing so hard that he's become disoriented. Where are his skis? He's sure they were right here, on the side of the trail, near that rock. But now they're gone. Or is it the wrong rock? Did he somehow make a turn and leave the trail? He doesn't think so, but in these conditions he can't be certain.

He can't believe it. He is wandering, alone, lost, and snow-blind, trying to find his skis. This is really annoying. He's going to be really pissed if he loses them. And his friends are going to be really mad that's he's late.

Without warning, he seems to float for a split second, then suddenly fall. Straight down, snow rushing up on both sides, scrambling to grab at something but finding only soft snow. He hears, then feels his ski boots crack through the layer of ice covering a frozen stream at the bottom of a crevasse. Dazed but fortunately uninjured, he's up to his shins in freezing cold water. He looks up, seeing only walls of white on all sides and the flakes gently cascading down into his hole from the evening sky above.

It's only an instant later that, for the first time, he begins to scream.

◉

Down at the Alpine Meadows base lodge, his friends are getting worried. It's after four o'clock and there is still no sign of Bennet. With conditions worsening and daylight fading fast, the group decides to alert the Ski Patrol, who begin a flurry of phone and radio calls. Lieutenant Chal DeCecco, Assistant Sub-Station Commander of the Lake Tahoe Sheriff's Office, takes charge of organizing the search and immediately activates the Incident Command System, or ICS.

The ICS, put in place by the state of California for just such time-sensitive emergencies, allows DeCecco to take command of a broad cross section of search and rescue groups. Within minutes, calls go out to all available emergency personnel: the California Highway Patrol, the Placer County and El Dorado County sheriff's offices, the Tahoe Nordic Search & Rescue Team, the U.S. Forest Service, the Marin County Wilderness Finders Search Dog Team, the Naval Air Station in Fallon, Nevada, and the Marine Corps Mountain Warfare Training Center, based near Bridgeport, California. Even nonemergency personnel are asked to help, lending the search teams their private Thiocols, wide-tracked snow groomers that can traverse steep terrain. De-Cecco commandeers one of the resort's outbuildings and sets up his tactical center, making sure he has radio contact with all the various personnel now suddenly under his command.

At 5:30 P.M. sixty rescuers, plus the avalanche dogs, set out into the night, scouring the area. Unfortunately, their search capability will be severely limited. Visibility is virtually nonexistent, and the temperature is dropping rapidly. Because of the deadly conditions, DeCecco decides that all helicopters are grounded until further notice.

◉

After ten or fifteen minutes of yelling "Can anyone hear me?" Bennet begins to realize that not only is no one coming but if he doesn't find a way out of the crevasse and the icy stream flowing through it, he will freeze to death. But as he gazes up at the sheer sides above him, he sees that climbing out will not be easy. The walls are not rock or ice—either of which might offer a hard surface to grip—but rather towering stacks of fluffy snow, which turns to dust in his gloves. Looking around for rocks or tree branches that might help him, and finding neither, he peers up at the edge of the hole and for the first time notices an overhanging branch. If he can just get up five or six feet, he may be able to grab the branch and swing his body out of the crevasse.

With no other choice, and darkness falling fast, he begins. Carving a few inches from the snowbank with his glove, he sticks just the tip of his right ski boot into the light powder. Shifting the weight of his body onto his right foot, he tests the indentation. It holds! Digging two small holes a foot above his head, he finds that he can put his hands in these, keep his balance, and then kick a new foothold with his free boot. With his hands and left foot now supporting his weight, he moves his right foot up, kicking a new hole. Using this laborious process, he finally makes it to the tree branch, grabs it, and heaves his body out into the snow. With his feet freezing but his body sweaty from the exertion, he collapses. Quickly the falling snow begins to cover him in a dusty layer of white.

With no watch, and no view of the horizon through the blizzard, he tries to determine how much light he has left. The climb took him about forty-five minutes, he figures, making it now close to 5:00 P.M., possibly later. Slowly the realization spreads over him: He has no choice but to spend the night and hope to make his way out the next morning. He must find some type of shelter. Now.

Wandering in the fading light, he stumbles across a large fallen tree in the woods with a dry spot underneath it. Grabbing his knees with his arms and pulling his hat down for warmth, he settles in for the night. But with his adrenaline flowing, sleep is impossible, and his mind drifts to his friends. Are they looking for him? Have they reported his absence? They must have, he surmises. He hears what he thinks are snowmobile engines in the distance. Are those the search teams? Maybe he should keep yelling.

The light fades, the storm blotting out the moonlight, leaving Bennet in total blackness. As he huddles on the cold ground under his tree, the snow continues to fall around him, rustling softly as it reaches some mysterious threshold and then collapses to the ground from the branches above. Soon he hears the ominous *whumps* of avalanche blasting, the detonations used by ski resorts to control snowslides. Though far away, the noises keep him on edge. Dejected but still reasonably optimistic, Bennet decides on a plan of action. In his mind, staying put means getting cold, and giving up. He will get moving, treat the whole thing as an adventure, as if he's G.I. Joe, forced to survive in crippling conditions using only his wits and his feet. *Whump!* Another blast.

He will make it! At first light, he will start hiking through the snow; it will probably have let up by then anyway. Figuring that he is somewhere mid-mountain, he decides he will simply hike down, assuming that this course will, eventually, take him to a base lodge. Yes, this is the plan. With a break in the weather and some good luck, he will run into a lift tower and follow the chairlift to civilization. Tomorrow, he'll be safe.

It is a strategy that will prove to have been badly miscalculated.

❖

The search and rescue mission for Bennet continues overnight, with little progress. The snow is coming down so hard that any tracks would have been covered hours ago, and the dogs are having trouble maneuvering in the deep, light powder. At some point in the night, Lieutenant DeCecco asks Bennet's friends if they have notified his parents. No one has. On the East Coast, a telephone rings in the middle of the night, and Bennet's mother answers. DeCecco explains the situation and hears a long scream at the other end of the line, then silence. A minute later Martin Zelner, Bennet's father, takes the phone and is told of his son's disappearance. Though he believes that Bennet is probably dead, DeCecco tells the young man's parents to hope for the best but prepare for the worst. He does not tell them that several years before another skier, also from back East, had gotten lost in the same area. Young and fit, like Bennet, he had wandered for miles. His badly decomposed body was found after the thaw, in a remote wilderness area called Hell Hole.

Thanking the lieutenant, a calm Martin Zelner hangs up and makes arrangements to fly to Chicago to pick up Emily, Bennet's sister. On Friday, Bill Borchard, Bennet's uncle, will fly to California, grimly prepared to collect his nephew's body.

◌

Thursday, January 5, dawns bitterly cold and blindingly white. Opening his eyes after a long, fitful night, Bennet is disheartened to see that the storm has not passed but rather has continued, even intensified. Feeling lousy, he stretches his legs, trying to get the blood flowing to his freezing toes. After several minutes he senses a burning pain in his chest: It's terrible heartburn, his stomach acid churning with nothing to digest. He's always been subject to the occasional bout, but this is like nothing he's felt before. The pain is so severe that moving is difficult. Trying to melt some snow for water to drink, he finds the powder so light and airy that its water content is minimal, forcing him to suck constantly on clumps just to keep his mouth from drying out. He tries his best to ignore the burning in his chest and prepares to move.

But to where? Frustrated by his inability to figure out where he is, he reconsiders his plan of the night before. Perhaps he should stay put and wait for rescue. He can still hear the occasional distant snowmobile engine, but no voices, and no dogs barking, and no helicopters. Maybe if he moves, he will enter an area that has already been searched, lessening his chances of being discovered. No, he finally decides, staying put means giving up. He is not going to give up.

Still confident that he can make his way down the mountain and, eventually, to an Alpine Meadows warming hut or lodge, he sets off.

And immediately sinks to his waist in snow.

❖

Alpine Meadows Ski Area offers some of the most challenging trails in the Sierra. But experts know that to ski the coveted "virgin" runs, the really deep, untouched powder, you must bypass the north side of the mountain and instead ski South Face and Big Bend, the steep, deep gulches on the far side of the resort. This area, called Sherwood Bowls, is accessed by first taking a chairlift to either Ward Peak or Scott Peak, the area's two summits, then skiing down the back face, serviced by the Sherwood and Lakeview chairlifts. These lifts are connected to each other by a short intermediate trail called Ray's Rut. Below the bases of the two lifts lies a single service road, then only wilderness. To return to the resort's restaurants and lodges, you must take one of the lifts back up and then ski down the front face of the mountain.

Unwittingly, Bennet had wandered off Ray's Rut and become disoriented. Because of his position relative to the main lifts, trails, and lodges of Alpine Meadows, he needed to be moving *up* the mountain, toward the summit ridge. Moving downhill would not, as he hoped, bring him to a developed area. Instead, it would send him into unpatrolled backcountry, the heavily wooded terrain of Tahoe National Forest, with virtually no inhabitants and no paved roads. Hiking in this direction was the worst possible choice he could have made.

In his zeal to save himself, Bennet had made another choice that would end up prolonging his ordeal. Determined to find his own way out of the wilderness, he kept moving, staying in one place only when darkness fell. While this reduced his feelings of helplessness—and as a result probably kept his spirits up—it also made it more difficult for searchers to find him. In fact, rescue personnel had reported crossing Bennet's tracks at least six times, only to find, each time, that they petered out.

○

When confronted with bad luck, what choices do we make, and why do we make them? How do these choices affect our mental (and in some cases our physical) state? These questions are especially appropriate in Bennet's case, since his choices ran counter to the advice from survival experts for those lost in the wilderness: Simply put, stay put, don't wander.

In attempting to counter his bad luck, Bennet was showing many of the signs of a condition mental health professionals call "illusory control." First identified by the Harvard psychologist Ellen Langer in the 1970s, illusory control is the belief that we are in control even when, objectively, we're not. Some common examples of this phenomenon deal with luck and chance. The lottery player who chooses his own number, or the gambler who insists on rolling his own dice, experiences the illusion of control over a random, uncontrollable situation. Illusory control is an adaptive measure that can increase motivation when one is facing difficult or adverse circumstances. It may make the player feel better about his chances, that his actions will cause a specific outcome, even when, from an observer's perspective, it is obvious that the event itself cannot be influenced.

In Bennet's mind, staying put meant giving up, and going on meant taking control of his fate. He had no way of knowing, of course, that wandering in the forest would take him farther from civilization. But while his illusory control may have delayed his rescue, it also helped him stay alive. It motivated him to action, which in itself tends to expand one's range of possibilities. It kept him searching, which kept him moving, which kept him warm. And, finally, it kept him busy and fended off depression and anxiety, both of which could have sapped his energy and his will to live.

In fact, his rescuers were constantly amazed at his energy level, expecting at virtually any moment to find his frozen body half-buried at the end of his footprints. But each time the footprints would disappear, filled in by the unceasing snow. Of Bennet, there was no sign. The trail had once again grown cold.

❃

Overnight, the snow has piled up at least another foot, and Bennet finds walking nearly impossible. He pulls one leg out of the powder, takes another step, and this time sinks to his waist. Each step is a grueling effort, and he requires several seconds of rest between tiny advances. With the snow falling in thick white sheets, he becomes disoriented. Isn't that the rock he just saw? Is that someone yelling? Is that a hut up ahead? Is he moving up the mountain or down? (Rescuers would later report following tracks that climbed, then descended, then climbed again.)

Confused, cold, thirsty, and terribly hungry, he keeps moving, more of a desperate, aimless wander than a purposeful hike. *He will go on. He will not stop. He will find his way out.* What's that? He notices a dull gleam on a tree. There's another! And it has a number on it! Markers! He's found some blazes! He keeps following the markings as if they are a trail (in fact they are Forest Service tree markers, not

trail markers), trying to maintain a downhill path. The wind is blowing so hard that the snow sounds as if it's rushing past him. No,
not the snow. Something else. Water. He hears water cascading over
rocks.

Bennet blasts out of the woods, sending snow spraying in front
of him as he half-runs, half-stumbles to the bank of a swollen stream.
The stream is flowing downhill, of course! All he has to do is follow
it and it will take him to the base lodge, or at least some sort of road
or bridge. Seeing that the other side appears slightly less wooded, he
decides to cross. But how? The stream is too wide, and the water is
flowing too fast to wade across. Anyway, the last thing he needs is to
be wetter; his toes are frozen as it is. He begins to hike with the
stream, following the curves of the bank until he sees a fallen tree
spanning the water. He climbs onto it and crawls across on hands and
knees. He's made it! But to what? It's the same terrain as the other
side. No, something looks, feels different. Then he sees it. There's a
gap in the woods, a white expanse without trees. A clearing.

Making his way to the field, he decides to carve HELP out of the
snow, in letters twenty feet across, as a signal to rescue planes or
choppers. The snow in the clearing is nearly chest deep, and carving
just the H—pushing the powder out of the way, stomping it down—
has exhausted him. But he finishes, hoping that a searcher in a helicopter will see his distress sign. That is, assuming a helicopter could
fly in these conditions. He peers up at the sky. The snow is still falling,
fast. He turns and looks back at his message. The huge trenches he
carved just minutes before are already being silently refilled.

Determined not to give up hope, Bennet feels that he must be
nearing the bottom of the mountain. The terrain seems to be slightly
flatter, with more clearings. Even more promising, he thinks he sees

lift towers off in the middle distance. With his glasses in his pocket and the thick curtain of snow, he can't be certain, of course, but he feels that he must be close to civilization. He decides he will continue hiking down, all night if necessary, until he finds his way out—or someone finds him.

But soon, as the moderate sunlight filtering through the snow starts to disappear, Bennet realizes that hiking at night is very foolish, and anyway simply will not be possible. Blackness in the mountains is complete. He decides he'd better find shelter again, while he still can. Noticing a large tree near the edge of a clearing, he carves out a small spot under it and curls up. Listening intently for voices, dogs barking, snowmobile engines, even avalanche blasting, he hears only the snow settling around him and the wind rustling the pine needles in the trees above him. He is hungry, tired, and freezing, afraid to take off his gloves and boots for fear of what he might see.

As his second night in the wilderness closes in around him, Bennet finds it difficult to focus his thoughts; his mind drifts. He thinks about the homeless who sleep in the freezing streets at night, about Holocaust survivors and the torments they survived for years. He knows that his body can withstand incredible hardship, but that if he doesn't keep a positive mental attitude, if he gives up hope or stops believing in himself, he won't make it. He will die out here in the woods, utterly, completely alone. But it can't end this way. It just can't. This is not his fate, he feels sure. He will make it out.

❉

Friday arrives cold but with hope. Bennet opens his eyes at dawn and immediately knows something is different. The quality of the light around him has changed. He is no longer in the hazy half-light of a snowstorm but rather in glorious, blindingly bright daylight, the sun reflecting off the coating of white all around him. Buoyed by the change in the weather, he begins to move but finds that he has trouble with his legs. The blood does not seem to be flowing to his feet, or his hands. He finds it hard to walk, stumbling about in the deep snow, in places up to his neck. Still, he manages to keep moving, hoping to come across a rescuer on a snowmobile or some shelter.

After about two hours of grueling, painful wandering, he hears a new sound, the low droning of an engine. He looks to the sky and sees an airplane. It's a commercial jet, much too high to see him, he knows. But still, this means that it's safe to fly!

Emboldened, he realizes that he needs to find some way of signaling. A fire! Remembering the lighter in his pocket, he pulls off his gloves. What he sees causes him to cringe. His hands are a sickly shade of yellow, his fingers puffy and badly swollen. He tries to manipulate the lighter, attempting to light a sapling, and fails. Dejected, with little energy left and hunger clawing at his belly, he stands at the edge of a clearing, trying to think clearly. He feels that he cannot hike any further, not with the snow so deep and his level of exhaustion.

Almost without realizing it, he finds himself looking to the sky. He's heard something, not the whiny buzzing of a snowmobile engine but something else, louder and deeper, more rhythmic. Then, above the tree line, he sees it, a small helicopter with CHP markings, hovering just overhead. With his last ounce of energy, he begins screaming, scratching his parched throat as he yells *Help!* over and over again. Waving his arms, trying to jump up and down in the deep snow, he continues yelling until, for some reason, the helicopter begins to move. *It's flying away! No!*

❖

At about the same time Bennet sees blue sky above, Lieutenant Chal DeCecco sees his launch window open. Knowing that the weather report is calling for another storm later in the day, he immediately orders his birds up: two helicopters from Fallon NAS, one from the CHP, and one from the Marines take off at his command. The helos will crisscross the mountain, searching for tracks or flashes of clothing. Looking at the clouds gathering to the west, DeCecco decides that, when the weather turns again, the search will be called off. He simply can't risk the lives of his personnel. Hearing the rotors of the choppers begin their slow winding up, he says a silent prayer. Then he goes inside, out of the cold.

❖

Exhausted, Bennet ponders his next move. He has not been rescued. His plan has failed. Worse, he's beginning to question his ability to go on, and his choices. Did he make the right decision to move rather than stay put? Would he have been found under that first tree? Standing there at the edge of the clearing, looking into the woods, he begins to realize that his energy has faded. Without food, he knows, there is no way he can hike through the deep snow for much longer. His hands—and, he assumes, his feet—are dangerously frostbitten, and the cold is slowly sapping any remaining heat from his body. If only the helicopter had seen him.

Minutes pass. With his glasses in his pocket, he looks out into the distance, objects nothing more than a white blur. Then movement catches his eye, something white against the white background, moving slowly but steadily toward him. *A rabbit!* Perhaps he can trap and kill it, and give himself some much-needed sustenance. But as the object moves closer, his eyes focus, and he realizes that what he sees is not a rabbit but a white helmet, on the head of a woman. On snowshoes, she is slowly, ponderously making her way on top of the snow through the forest toward him. When she is close enough to be heard, she says, "You don't know how happy I am to see you."

For the first time in two days, Bennet smiles.

He's made it out alive.

◉

The woman, Flight Officer and Paramedic Leslie Berndl of the California Highway Patrol's Valley Division Air Operations Unit, explains that the CHP helicopter Bennet had seen could not touch down in the deep snow and had found a suitable landing site a short hike away. With Bennet unable to navigate through the snow, a Marine rescue helicopter is called in. After signaling their position via rescue flares, Officer Berndl stays behind while Bennet is hoisted aboard the huge dual-rotor chopper. He is put into a hypothermia bag and flown to a municipal airfield, then taken in an ambulance to Tahoe Forest Hospital in Truckee. First, he is treated for hypothermia, placed in a warming tub until his core temperature can be raised. He calls his mother and tells her he is okay. She is overcome and begins to cry.

By this time the hospital is packed with reporters, and Bennet is asked if he feels up for a brief press conference. He agrees, but only after trading in his flowery hospital gown for a more appealing blue surgeon's shirt. His voice breaking, he thanks those who risked their own lives to save his and gives a few details of his ordeal. The rescuers add some words. Lieutenant DeCecco says, "We were all fortunate to get the break in the weather and have had a massive team effort." Says Placer County Sheriff's Sergeant John FitzGerald: "It was just amazing luck. I'm sure he would not have survived another night." FitzGerald pauses, then adds, "It's not hit him yet, but it will. He's very lucky."

◉

Though he is indeed lucky to be alive, Bennet is informed that his medical condition is serious. As he had suspected, both his hands and his feet are badly frostbitten. When they thaw, the doctors tell him, he will be in terrible pain, for days and possibly even weeks. He is given morphine and Halcion for the pain, and as a result drifts in and out of hazy consciousness, spending two days in intensive care and another day in the general ward. Dr. Howard Boone, a frostbite specialist, recommends against amputating any damaged skin. Instead, he and Bennet decide to wait to see if the nerve endings regenerate. Slowly, they do, and he feels first sharp needles, then burning fire, then a dull throbbing ache. When he returns to school a few weeks later, Bennet is forced to use a wheelchair, and then crutches, until his feet heal.

The story does not end there, however. Shortly after his rescue, Bennet is approached by a television producer. Would he be interested in telling his story for *Real Stories of the Highway Patrol,* one of the earliest low-budget "reality" TV shows? Since he had been rescued by a CHP chopper, the producer tells Bennet, the story is perfect for the program. Happy to grab another fifteen minutes of fame—he's actually enjoying all the attention—Bennet quickly agrees to be interviewed.

Some months later Bennet's friends throw a "Real Stories" party for him, complete with three televisions, snacks, and plenty of beer. Lots of people show up to watch his harrowing ordeal given the reality-show treatment, even though they know the footage will be nothing but reenactments. Bennet is excited. He can't wait to see how Hollywood portrays his climb from the crevasse, his nights alone in the forest, and his long hike through the woods to the clearing where he was finally sighted.

Unfortunately, he will be disappointed, and embarrassed. The show portrays him as a hapless daredevil, a gung ho college kid who is dumb enough to ski into a blizzard and so helpless that he gives up almost immediately rather than seek rescue. At one point he is even shown curled up in the snow in the fetal position. It is only through the bravery of the intrepid California Highway Patrol helicopter pilot, battling the elements, that the lost skier is plucked from the jaws of death and returned to his grateful family.

Bennet's luck, the program seems to imply, was limited to the good luck that he was found. The rest of his story was nothing more than carelessness and hubris.

◉

Clearly, Bennet Zelner made mistakes. He skied alone. He skied in unfamiliar territory. He didn't tell anyone where he was going. And, at least when viewed objectively (and with the benefit of hindsight), his aimless wandering prolonged his ordeal. He was also on the receiving end of some very bad luck where the weather was concerned. He happened to get lost at the beginning of one of the worst blizzards during one of the worst winters in California history. The snow happened to be very light, making melting it for water difficult, and navigating through it particularly exhausting. When the weather finally changed, his luck changed, too. The clouds parted, he was spotted, and he was saved.

But when he was faced with bad luck, Bennet's decision to take some measure of control, rather than rely on others, was probably the right choice. Research on depression and control supports this view: While some people will have runs of good and bad luck, ability and effort generally produce more good outcomes and fewer bad ones than would happen otherwise. This perspective also helps to explain his anger with *Real Stories,* which incorrectly created the impression that he had no control over his situation. In research studies, the absence of control—whether over good outcomes or bad—is associated with depression.

As Bennet discovered, bad luck can't be predicted. But its effects can be contained, especially in situations where we can maintain a measure of control—even if that control is, on the whole, illusory—over what happens to us. By staying in control, by wandering until he found that clearing, Bennet put himself in a position to capitalize on good luck when it appeared through the clouds, as if sent from above.

CHAPTER 3

A Cardboard Box with Airholes
and a Carrying Handle

The bar is loud. And it's smoky. And Gary Dahl has already con-
sumed one too many—at least.

It's a cool April evening in 1975, and the Grog and Sirloin in Los
Gatos, California, is buzzing. Elton John's "Philadelphia Freedom" is
playing on the jukebox; it's recently hit number 1 on the *Billboard*
chart, surpassing Minnie Riperton's "Lovin' You." Gary, dressed in
his typical bell-bottom plaid trousers and tight, wide-collared shirt, is
chatting at a corner table with some fellow advertising copywriters.
At forty his hair is still blond and his full beard has not yet gone gray,
though it will soon. With his quick wit and sharp mind, he's had
some moderate success in the field, doing mostly small campaigns
for local radio and TV. But, as always, things could be better.

The recession that began in '73 is in full swing, with the bull
market of 1969 through 1972 now a distant memory; the Dow is still

inching up from a low of under 600 the previous December. While the oil crisis of 1973–74 is finally over, prices at the pump are still about 20 percent higher than they were, and combined with a stagnant economy and staggering 14 percent inflation, making a living is tougher than ever. Things are so bad that Gary has started driving a Honda Civic, a small import relatively rare at the time, because it gets more miles to the gallon. For everyone, it seems, money is tight.

It makes some sense, then, that the conversation turns from advertising to the high cost of living. Sure, California is a great place to live, they all agree, if you don't mind driving everywhere. And with gas at nearly sixty cents a gallon, just getting to work is costing an arm and a leg these days. And the smog? It's worse than ever.

At some point in the evening, the conversation shifts to the high cost of pet ownership. Dogs, Gary notes, are particularly expensive, what with the food, the shots, the grooming, and especially obedience school. After all, what is the point of a dog that can't do tricks on command? Plus they are messy. While at a bookstore, on a whim he'd picked up a few of the newest crop of dog training manuals, he mentions. He found them hilarious, with their silly advice and hyperserious tone. Does anyone actually read those things?

As the group discusses the financial pros and cons of fish, hamsters, cats, and even rabbits, a phrase suddenly pops into his head. Without thinking, he blurts it out.

"What about a pet rock?"

❀

It's been said that necessity is the mother of invention. But what if you invented something that nobody needed, and people still bought it—by the millions? To what would you attribute your success? The answer, it seems, is luck, and some pretty amazing timing. Such is the incredible success story of Gary Dahl's Pet Rock, a novelty item that sold more than a million units in a six-month period in 1975 and became a cultural phenomenon.

While everyone knows what the Pet Rock was, few understand what it was meant to be: according to Gary Dahl, an entirely new way to package and sell a paperback book. This, and not a small piece of ordinary Rosarita Beach landscaping stone, was the true genius behind the fad. From the flash of a thought at a hole-in-the-wall saloon to an important slice of Americana, the metamorphosis of the Pet Rock from idea to icon can teach us much about how luck and timing interact. But the story is also illustrative of the importance of being able to act on an idea quickly, to move before the moment is gone and your luck runs out.

◉

Who would buy a Pet Rock? Gary Dahl isn't sure, but it doesn't really matter, because it's not a rock that he's planning to sell. Rather, he hopes, it's his spoof of a dog training manual, which he's been working on for a few weeks now, ever since that night at the Grog and Sirloin. After he shared his Pet Rock concept that night, he and his friends had thrown around ideas, trying out gags, thinking of one-liners and tag lines, making up imaginary ad copy for this new "maintenance-free" pet. But while they were at home nursing hangovers, Gary was in the zone, doing what he does best: brainstorming, jotting down notes, mentally considering and then rejecting ideas, ordering and then reordering paragraphs and chapters.

After a few days, things begin to gel, and Gary starts to organize his concept. The book will be called *The care and training of your PET*

ROCK. It should be as close to a true dog training manual as possible, with an introduction on "acclimating" your Pet Rock to its new home. The text will play it very straight:

> Your new rock is a very sensitive pet and may be slightly traumatized from all the handling and shipping required in bringing the two of you together. Some Pet Rock owners have found that the ticking of an alarm clock placed near the box has a soothing effect; especially at night.

He decides to include chapters on obedience ("A rock that doesn't come when it's called will cause its owner endless embarrassment"), tricks ("Play Dead. Your Pet Rock will take to this trick like a duck takes to water"), and health ("Blood out of a rock. If you are getting blood out of your rock you should contact the Internal Revenue Service immediately. They've been attempting to do this very thing for years"). Rather than being overtly humorous, Gary feels, the book will work more stealthily; laughs should come not from obvious jokes but rather from the seriousness of the tone and the absurdity of the concept. It should have some basic illustrations, nothing too detailed.

But how to sell it? As an adman, Gary knows the importance of marketing, of selling the sizzle, not just the steak. He also knows, though, that a good pitch isn't enough. What he needs is a clever package, something that will both sell the product inside and play on the consumer's notion of what buying a pet actually means. Then he remembers the pet carriers that people use to bring animals to and from the vet, and he's got it. He talks to a friend in the calendar business, and the two of them design a prototype "Pet Rock carrier," a cardboard box with airholes in the sides and a handle. The rock itself will sit on a bed of strawlike excelsior, Gary decides, and the carrier will be big enough to hold a rock, the bedding, and his book.

There's just one problem. The book is almost a hundred pages long. Figuring that no one is likely to read a Pet Rock training manual that is the length of an actual dog obedience book, he decides to cut it to a more manageable forty pages. This length, he surmises, is long enough to maintain the conceit but not so long that a reader will get tired and the jokes will grow stale. To keep costs down, he decides to print the book in "pocket" format, about three inches long and two inches wide.

It's now August and, with a carload of prototype Pet Rocks ready to go, he drives to a gift show in San Francisco, where he has rented table space. The show attendees consist primarily of department store and gift store buyers, as well as a few media types. With absolutely no inkling of how his creation will be received, Gary takes out his order pad and sets up his table full of prototype Pet Rock carriers. Then he waits.

✻

In 1975 the adult novelty market was still relatively small. "Novelty gifts at that time were pretty much limited to chattering teeth and the whoopee cushion," Gary recalls. Indeed, novelties had been intended for and marketed to kids, not grown-ups, for the better part of the twentieth century. One man in particular, Soren Sorensen Adams (known as Sam), had single-handedly created the market in 1905 with his invention and marketing of sneezing powder. Adams's coal-tar powder was many times more potent than pepper, and just three months after its introduction, he sold seventy thousand bottles of his concoction (known as Cachoo) to a single Philadelphia retailer. In a lesson that Gary Dahl was to learn firsthand nearly seventy years later, Sam's invention was almost immediately pirated. Sam Adams moved on to invent other classic novelty gags such as the Snake Jam Jar, the Dribble Glass, the Shiner, and the Joy Buzzer.

Though Gary did not know it at the time, the novelty market in 1975 was ripe for the Pet Rock—or at least a gag gift like it that appealed to adults, not just kids. The store most directly responsible for the modern novelty gift boom is Spencer Gifts, which was undergoing rapid expansion in the 1970s. Founded just after World War II by Max Adler as a catalog company in Easton, Pennsylvania, Spencer Gifts opened its first retail store in 1963 in Cherry Hill, New Jersey. Fueled by the huge number of cheap plastic dolls, toys, and games coming to market in the 1950s and '60s, Spencer Gifts began opening stores across the country. When it was acquired by Universal Studios (then MCA) in 1968, the chain had grown exponentially, and hundreds of stores would open in the decade from 1970 to 1980. The stores carried not just children's toys and novelties but more expensive and adult-themed gifts, like Lava lamps and adult joke books.

The national psyche, too, was primed for a cheap, humorous gift concept and in dire need of some levity. Upon the fall of Saigon in April 1975, the war in Vietnam had ended with U.S. Marines airlifting nationals out of the embassy in advance of North Vietnamese troops. More than 58,000 Americans had been killed, with three times that many injured, and the country was still reeling from the deeply divisive conflict. Moreover, President Richard Nixon's resignation was still fresh in the minds of many, his departure to avoid impeachment nearly a year old. Combined with the dire economic situation, these events helped to create a cultural and social climate of general malaise and dispiritedness. The most successful movie of the year, *Jaws,* was about death from below, while the 1975 Pulitzer Prize–winning novel, *The Killer Angels,* was about death on the Civil War battlefields. It seemed the entire country could use a good laugh.

○

Gary the adman is bemused, sitting there at a table covered with Pet Rocks at a San Francisco gift show. Looking over his collection of rocks, he wonders what he was thinking, trying to sell the public on a crazy book wrapped in a clever package. But then something odd happens. The slow trickle of people stopping by turns into a steady stream. Gift buyers are reading his book and laughing out loud. They are grabbing colleagues, bringing them over to the table. Many are taking notes, asking him about price, quantities, ship dates. Soon the stream turns into a torrent, and the table is so crowded that they're lining up to get a look at the Pet Rock. He's taking orders as fast as he can write, scribbling down the names of buyers and stores while all the time hawking the Pet Rock to passersby.

By the end of the day, Gary is exhausted. As he packs up the car, he stops to check his order pad; he's been so busy he hasn't kept track of his sales. When he tallies up the numbers, he can scarcely believe it. He's got orders for five thousand units! The following month Gary attends the New York gift show and gets orders for five thousand more Pet Rocks. He knows he has a hot product on his hands.

Gary has decided that he wants to clear a dollar per unit, so he gives the Pet Rock a suggested retail price of four to five dollars. He's already made a tidy sum, certainly more than he'd hoped. But now he's got to figure out a way to quickly, efficiently, and (most important) inexpensively assemble and distribute thousands of units of his concept. Since his book has no publisher, he also needs enough cash to cover his out-of-pocket expenses.

With the assistance of a friend at an ad agency, Gary is able to secure a line of credit, giving him enough money to cover printing, assembly, and shipping costs. But with the orders pouring in, he needs help; he can't possibly fill them all by himself. He eventually finds an agency that provides temporary workers to the fledgling computer business in nearby San Jose. The temps are accustomed to highly detailed assembly work—mostly assembling circuit boards—so putting the boxes together and stuffing them should be no problem. The company will warehouse the finished Pet Rock carriers and handle order fulfillment, charging Gary a minuscule twelve cents per unit. To get the Pet Rocks to market as quickly as possible, Gary decides to use United Parcel Service, which costs more than the Postal Service; he figures he'll make up the extra expense through larger volume. (In 1975 Federal Express was just two years old, and too expensive to be feasible for such a cheap product, though now Gary speculates that a cheap overnight shipping option probably would have allowed him to double his sales volume.)

In October, as the Pet Rocks begin hitting store shelves, Gary receives a call from a buyer for Neiman Marcus, the high-end retail chain and catalog company. Would he be interested in a small "test order" for their flagship Dallas store? He quickly agrees and slips the information into his press release. The release is soon picked up by *Newsweek,* and the magazine gives the Pet Rock a half-page story, including the Neiman Marcus details. Almost immediately the store gets thousands of orders, and Gary's little gag gift starts to change, going from frivolity to phenomenon in a span of weeks. By late October, Gary is moving ten thousand Pet Rocks a day, and as with all fads the media are driving as well as reporting sales. ("It was a media event as much as a sales event," Gary remembers.) With the national press fanning the flames, he begins fielding hundreds of interview requests. Walter Cronkite, announcing in his hyperserious voice that "we don't normally do stories like this," reports on the Pet Rock on the *CBS Evening News*. John Davidson, substitute hosting for Johnny Carson on *The Tonight Show,* brings a Pet Rock onstage. Sales skyrocket, and a fad is born.

Then the knockoffs begin flooding the market.

Gary had the foresight to copyright his book and trademark "Pet Rock" before shipping a single unit. These precautions were smart, but they are not effective in protecting his concept. Fly-by-night operations begin cropping up almost immediately. They start copying Gary's idea and selling the Pet Rock and the training manual—in some cases reproducing the book verbatim. "Copyright and trademark allow you to sue," Gary says years later, "but they can't prevent someone from selling a knockoff." Indeed, Gary decides to file suit against a Seattle-based company that is having huge success selling pirated Pet Rocks. But the company soon closes up shop and disappears, leaving him with a large judgment in his favor but not a dime in damages. ("I really wish I had all the money back that I spent on lawyers," he recalls.)

But even with pirates selling nearly as many Pet Rocks as Gary is, his profits continue to climb. By Christmas 1975, sales have reached more than a million units. The Pet Rock is officially a cult phenomenon. And Gary is a rich man.

But as 1975 draws to a close, he sees his wild ride begin to end.

After the holiday season, sales of the Pet Rock taper off. Possibly all the media attention oversaturated the market, making the Pet Rock a victim of its own success. Or perhaps all the knockoffs finally began to take their toll, and consumers had seen just one Pet Rock too many. Whatever the reason, when Gary tries to remarket the concept for Valentine's Day 1976, the Pet Rock fails miserably. The fad has run its course, and after a whirlwind six months, Gary's amazing luck has finally run out.

His success has damaged some friendships, particularly with those who were at the Grog and Sirloin that fateful April night. "They were angry, and they were jealous," Gary remembers, and many wanted to get in on the luck. "They were mad that I had capitalized on an idea that we had all discussed that night. But I was the one who went home and worked on the Pet Rock for two weeks, while they just forgot about it."

✦

In addition to some lucky timing, why was the Pet Rock such a success? Are there other kinds of forces that work to create a pop-culture fad? Malcolm Gladwell, a science writer and the author of *The Tipping Point,* has studied social phenomena and believes that in many ways they behave like traditional medical epidemics. "Ideas and products and messages and behaviors spread just like viruses do," he says. Gladwell believes that for small ideas and products to spread widely and with tremendous speed, a particular kind of person needs to pick up on them. Such people may have a highly diverse set of social or business connections, or may themselves be powerful enough to broadly influence public opinion.

Did one of these people stumble upon the Pet Rock, helping to spread the news far and wide, and in a hurry? Perhaps, but the impact and importance of the extensive media coverage of Gary's Pet Rock cannot be overstated. According to one reckoning, by Christmas 1975 three-quarters of all daily newspapers in the United States had run Pet Rock stories, creating what was in essence a free advertising campaign that reached tens of millions of potential buyers. The media's impact, however, while important, came after Gary had already sold tens, perhaps hundreds, of thousands of units. What sparked the initial buying frenzy?

Perhaps the gift buyers at the two trade shows were responsible. As Gladwell suggests, this select group of people may have had broad enough professional and social connections that they were able to push the Pet Rock beyond its "tipping point," turning a gift into a fad almost overnight. Maybe they were the ones who brought the concept to the masses, via department store chains and small gift stores. Another possible suspect (or more accurately suspects) are the well-off shoppers of the trendy Neiman Marcus stores. Perhaps the appearance of the Pet Rock at this upmarket retail titan lent it some cachet in more rarefied social circles, giving it the sheen of cool and thereby expanding its reach and widening its potential market. After all, if even the country club set was talking about the Pet Rock, it had to be all the rage.

Although it's difficult to codify the reasons behind a pop-culture fad, science may also help in understanding why some products (and people) get lucky while others do not. A recent study in the *Journal of Consumer Research* has found that emotional contagion, or the transferring of emotions from one person to another, can result from something as minor (and unconscious) as a smile or a laugh. Such positive reinforcement and the exchange of positive attitudes are especially prevalent if the consumers like one another, and may be responsible for explaining the effectiveness of word-of-mouth communication. Gary's Pet Rock combined an entertaining concept with a humorous book and a funny package, making it an excellent source of positive emotional feedback. It's highly likely that such emotional contagiousness "infected" people as they watched others enjoy the Pet Rock concept.

It's obvious that Gary benefited from a number of lucky breaks in his Pet Rock success. The sour economy made a cheap gift appealing. Political and military failures contributed to a climate of melancholy, opening the door for humor. The decision to market the Pet Rock as a gift, rather than as a book, helped spread the word far beyond mainstream publishing circles and bookstores. Gift and novelty stores were rapidly expanding at the time. And, of course, the relentless media attention solidified the Pet Rock as a true pop-cultural symbol.

But in a sense Gary Dahl contributed to his own luck. At the Grog and Sirloin that April night after a few too many drinks, he decided to take a chance on an idea. He could not have known how things would turn out, but he believed in his idea, and in his ability to turn an idea into something concrete. And that was enough. He had some very lucky breaks along the way—friends who made suggestions, business contacts who helped get the necessary funding—but he had put himself in a position to capitalize when the breaks came along. And when he began to see that his prototype Pet Rock was selling well at the gift shows, Gary made some fast, risky, and important decisions (lining up financing, securing temp workers) that allowed him to take advantage of his phenomenal luck when sales of the Pet Rock skyrocketed.

Gary's story may appear to be simply one lucky event after another, but recent studies have shown that believing in an initial stroke of luck can pave the way for future success, success based on skill, not luck. Indeed, research indicates that a belief in good luck can have some highly beneficial consequences. The marketing and psychology expert Peter Darke of the University of British Columbia has shown that people who experience initial "good luck" events perform better on subsequent, subjectively unrelated tasks.

The precise mechanisms that cause such increased performance are not yet known. But it is thought that experiencing good luck makes people more confident in their abilities and gives them a greater sense of control. "The superstitious feeling that 'luck is on one's side' can make a difference [in] circumstances where one's mental attitude counts because a feeling of confidence can affect performance," writes the philosopher Nicholas Rescher. Thus, taking advantage of a piece of good luck—no matter how minor—may in fact open doors that would otherwise have remained closed.

As silly as it sounds, the Pet Rock was an idea whose time had come. But what if it wasn't just a product of the 1970s? Could the Pet Rock be reissued and sold successfully today? One company thought so. In 2000, the Fun-4-All Corp., a concern that licenses many novelty products, paid Gary a small sum for the rights to reprint his book, re-create the carrier, and sell his idea once again.

The result? The Pet Rock has languished, with only very modest sales. As Gary Dahl notes, it seems the joke has already been told.

CHAPTER 4

Jenny, I've Got Your Number

It's early in 1981, and Tommy Heath is in the studio, again, and he is getting frustrated.

The band has spent months recording the tracks for their second album; the process has gone on too long. Now they find out that Columbia, their CBS-owned record label, is unhappy with the first batch of songs. They need to rerecord, Columbia says, and with new material.

With the knowledge that it's been nearly a year since the release—and moderate success—of the band's first album, Tommy is getting nervous. The public, and the radio stations, has a short memory. They might miss that critical window of opportunity that will allow their music to build an audience, rather then peter out. The band's single from the first album, "Angel Say No," had charted in the Top 40 the year before but now was falling off playlists. Unless they came up with something soon, Columbia's marketing machine might give them some token publicity and then move on to the next band. Ruefully, Tommy thinks of the dozens of other bands that had been signed with them. Maybe ten had made it into the studio, and of those ten the label had released albums by only five. Would they be the next casualties?

At some point, as he fiddles with his guitar and tests out some new licks, Tommy sees that Jim has finally arrived. Jim Keller, his partner and the band's other guitarist, is carrying some sheet music and some scribbled lyrics. He appears to be excited. With the help of Alex Call, a local musician and his songwriting partner, he has come up with a song that has some potential. Would Tommy give it a try?

Tommy takes a look, his eyes scanning down the page to the chorus. That's funny, he thinks, I've never seen a chorus that's just a bunch of numbers. Slowly he realizes that the seven digits of the chorus make up a phone number, but not one he's ever heard before. It's an odd lyric, admittedly, but no more odd than some of the other stuff they'd written.

He clears his throat, and then, in his low, distinctive twang, singing forcefully, he gives the line a shot: "Eight six seven, five three oh nine."

Yeah, he thinks. It works.

*

How does a song become a hit? What makes a band a "one-hit wonder"? How does luck operate in the music world, where the vagaries of taste can make—or quickly and cruelly break—a song, a star, even a career?

In the modern recording industry, successful songs—and stars—

are generally not discovered but rather are manufactured, sculpted and shaped until they fit some mold predetermined by record company executives and their accountants. The current obsession with superchoreographed boy bands and blond teenage starlets in soda commercials results in hits that sound derivative, with minor tweaks added to whatever came just before in the hope of capturing the same listeners.

But one phenomenon of the recording industry has not changed over the years: the one-hit wonder, the artist with the lucky break, the musician who moves to the top of the charts only to fall suddenly, never to return. From "Radar Love" to "In-A-Gadda-Da-Vida," from "Macarena" to "Ice Ice Baby," songs have continued to appear, become ubiquitous, then quickly disappear with regularity, despite the attempts of artists (and their labels) to build on success and create a series of hits. Such artists are often described as "victims of their own success," frustratingly unable to re-create the particular set of circumstances that led to their rise. Are these artists responsible for their own good (and subsequent bad) luck, or are other, more uncontrollable factors at work? What causes a song to become a phenomenon, then fade into oblivion? And how do the one-hit wonders view their sudden—and fleeting—fame?

Inevitably, the luck that creates a one-hit wonder is a complex series of events, only some of which are musical in nature. A one-hit wonder may, when viewed objectively, be a good song (though of course music tastes are highly subjective). But it may also be a bad song so universally loathed that it gains in popularity despite (or because of) its awfulness. More often than not, social and cultural shifts—including changes in listening patterns, new fashions, new technology, even weather—are equally responsible for the rise of a particular song. The hit of the record-setting hot summer of 2002 was Nelly's "Hot in Herre." Though such shifts are generally impossible to predict, savvy musicians and the record companies who can spot them early and capitalize through targeted publicity stand a better chance of moving up the charts quickly, before factors change.

Another important aspect of luck in the music business is the formation of a core group of musicians, managers, and promoters who can make sure that songs are heard on the radio, essential for any hit. If a key person in the group loses interest or is replaced, a song can easily fall by the wayside, replaced by any one of a hundred competitors. Without such a group, musicians with a hit song generally become one-hit wonders, unable to get new material the necessary exposure. Furthermore, the pressures that come with success are often the death knell for soon-to-be one-hit wonders. Bands try too hard, or take too long, or rush through a follow-up effort, and it falls flat. And, inevitably, band members are distracted by money and are unable to concentrate on their music.

From a broader perspective, the fortunes and misfortunes of the one-hit wonder can tell us much about how luck operates in a group dynamic, where relationships can quickly be swayed by sudden success—or failure. Recent research indicates that, in dynamic industries like the arts, success and fame may owe more to a broad range of relatively loose and fluid relationships than to a small number of longer-lasting associations.

This so-called weak-tie theory holds that the experience of individuals is closely bound to other issues relating to their social structure, and that weak ties are indispensable to each individual's opportunities. Further, changes in personnel or in the overall network (both positive and negative) can, over time, have serious consequences for those with ties to the person or group.

Weak ties also allow an individual to interact with a wide range of people who have different professional interests and social associations, which expands opportunity. This is important, since most people are likely to have stronger, more lasting relationships with those who are more similar to themselves, limiting the opportunity to meet others with different sets of associations. In this context, a luck event can influence, and be influenced by, both relatively minor social relationships and larger cultural shifts that alter the makeup of one's professional associations.

All of these issues—and many more besides—factor into the story of "867-5309" and Tommy Tutone, a talented eighties band that came along at just the right time, yet ultimately failed to capitalize on a gold single that resulted from an amazing streak of luck.

❖

The late 1970s was a time of change in the San Francisco rock music scene. While traditional "jam" bands like the Grateful Dead and the Allman Brothers Band continued to play to packed rooms, rock was undergoing something of a two-way transformation. In one direction, early heavy metal supergroups like Led Zeppelin, AC/DC, and Van Halen were giving music a harder edge. This change set the stage for the arrival of the Punk invasion, personified by the Clash and, especially, the Sex Pistols, who played their first (and only) San Francisco show in 1978. The Fillmore Auditorium, the promoter Bill Graham's legendary venue for seminal sixties rock bands like the Jimi Hendrix Experience, Jefferson Airplane, and Santana, had closed in the early seventies, while Winterland, the old San Francisco ice-skating rink that served to replace it, would shut its doors late in 1978.

In the other direction, folk-based singer-songwriters like James Taylor and Linda Ronstadt were bringing their mellow blend of blue-grass and country to audiences who had partied through the sixties—and had no desire to go back. And, above all, disco was ruling the airwaves and the charts, limiting the radio exposure of rock, traditional R & B, and folk artists alike.

It was about this time that a new genre of music began to develop, one that was given the name New Wave because, ostensibly, it was different from anything that had come before. In fact, New Wave was simply an outgrowth of Punk, perhaps best thought of as Punk Light. "People were tired of the sneers, the attitude of Punk, but they liked the aggressive feel of the music," says Stephen "Spaz" Schnee, a twenty-year veteran of the music business and New Wave evangelist. "New Wave developed from bands that had been known as 'pub bands,'" Schnee adds, "basically guys with long hair who were playing country-ish songs, bands like Cheap Trick. The music was melodic, but it still had the Punk spirit."

"Nineteen seventy-eight was the year that Mute Records, soon to be the home of Depeche Mode and many others, was founded by Daniel Miller, who had released the shocking and stark single 'Warm Leatherette' under the name 'The Normal,'" says Mike Paulsen, an expert on the New Wave music scene. "Nineteen seventy-eight was really the year that New Wave began taking off out of the ashes of the 'seventy-seven Punk explosion," he adds.

One band in particular, the Knack, moved to the forefront of the New Wave scene; they were Los Angeles's answer to East Coast bands like the Ramones and Blondie. "The Knack was the first big New Wave band in California, selling a million albums," Schnee says. "As a result there was this huge backlash, with people saying they sold out. For a while there was a brisk business in 'Nuke the Knack!' buttons."

The Knack may have been the biggest New Wave band in California, but there were many, many others. An influential independent label from San Francisco called 415 Records was promoting dozens of groups with the new, edgier sound, and bands like 20/20, the Tubes, Wire Train, and Great Buildings were drawing big crowds at their live shows, though most would break up within a few years. (The founders of Great Buildings, Danny Wilde and Phil Solem, however, would go on to form the Rembrandts, another one-hit wonder, best known now for the theme song of the TV show *Friends*.)

Today, New Wave is often associated with the skinny neckties of fashion-conscious front men wearing narrow-lapeled blazers and platform shoes, and indeed these were an indelible part of the genre. But more to the point, New Wave music took off because the sound combined the fast guitar and bass riffs of Punk and the groovy beats of the disco era to create modern, danceable music that was socially acceptable at clubs. New Wave also had a distinct "pop sensibility," different from the "rock sensibility" of other current artists, such as Bruce Springsteen.

❂

Tommy Heath, known as Tommy Tutone to his friends, had been a self-described hippie in the sixties and early seventies, living in Mendocino and working odd jobs. He had picked up guitar and some piano between painting jobs, tile work, and occasional student teaching, and found that he had some skill, both as a player and as a singer. By 1977 he had been in a succession of Bay Area bands but had soured on rock and roll, leading him to try a progression of sounds— folk, country, reggae—looking for one that fit his playing and singing style. His voice, a guttural twang that sounded a bit like a southern version of Elvis Costello, could cover a broad range of music with ease.

Early in 1978, Tommy decides to move to San Francisco, with the intention of taking up music full-time, either as a songwriter or as a studio musician. He is also looking to put together a bar band, but one with a different sound, something edgy, with hints of his various musical influences. For several weeks he sits in on jam sessions around the city, playing with musicians of different stripes, until one day his wife, Becky, mentions a young guitar player she has heard named Jim Keller. In his early twenties at the time, Jim—a self-described hippie guitarist—had moved out West from Vermont a few years before and was paying the rent by renovating old Victorians. A self-taught guitarist who could not read music, Jim has a unique style that appeals to Tommy, and the two immediately begin playing in frequent jam sessions.

Under the billing Tommy Tutone, the duo (with various backup musicians) secures regular gigs in local bars, including Uncle Charlie's in Marin County and the Keystone in Berkeley, occasionally playing to audiences of just five or six. "I had just bought my first electric guitar," Jim remembers years later. "And I didn't even have an amp. But Tommy saw something in me, I guess." Tommy had more of a country rock style than he did, Jim recalls, but he had a great voice and almost immediately became the front man. "I was apprehensive, I didn't think I was good enough to be up there, but Tommy had the presence onstage," Jim remembers. Both men are busy writing lots of material, and word begins to spread of their different sound, which some have called "power-pop," a mix of pub rock, soul, and country. At one point they even have an opening act, a young Bay Area band, growing in popularity, called Huey Lewis and the News.

By 1979, Tommy and Jim are well known enough to be invited to an important music event, a "label showcase" at the Keystone. The evening will feature a number of bands playing for recording industry A & R reps and powerful entertainment lawyers. The headliner will be a group called Rocky Sullivan, a short-lived band that took the name of its well-known San Francisco front man. The band also features a number of high-profile musicians, including John Cipollina, formerly of Quicksilver Messenger Service, and Nicky Hopkins, a talented studio player who had played keyboards for the Who and the Rolling Stones, among other bands. Tommy Tutone will be the opening act.

The band decides to do a varied set that will showcase the broad sound for which they are known. They play several of the songs that will appear on their demo, including "Sounds of a Summer Night," "Girl in the Back Seat," and "Rachel." They add a country tune that Tommy has written called "That's No Way to Cry," and a few of Jim's songs, including "Somebody's Leaving" and "Show Some Faith." (Tommy will later lament the fact that although these were some of the best tunes Jim had ever written, they never made it onto an album.) The songs are infused with great harmonies, catchy guitar riffs, and a strong vocal blend of lyrics and impromptu shouts and calls to the audience—plus Tommy's trademark gap-toothed grin. They close with a rowdy, Punk version of Cat Stevens's "Wild World," to raucous applause.

The show is a success, and it will bring several studios, including the powerful Warner Bros. label, calling within a month. However, the night will also spur a change in the band's sound, a change that will later be described by Tommy as their "deal with the devil." Mike Varney, a respected guitarist who had enjoyed the band's set, suggests that they narrow their focus, discarding the soul songs and country tunes that were often interspersed with their more poplike material. Tommy Tutone, it is suggested, would be an excellent "New Wave" band, one of the new breed of "crossovers," a pop band with an edgier side. Varney will not be the last person to make this recommendation. "We eventually fired our keyboard player, hired a Punk bass player, and put on some skinny ties" to fit in, Jim Keller says in retrospect.

The West Coast arm of Warner Bros. eventually agrees to pick up the tab for the studio time required to produce a Tommy Tutone demo tape. The demo will be recorded at the Automat, an old CBS studio in San Francisco. Lonnie Turner, who had played bass with the Steve Miller Band and cowritten the hit "Jungle Love" in 1977, will produce the tracks. The WB execs, however, feel that some of the material is too funky and ask the band to mellow their sound, preferring a less hard-edged version of the pub rock the band has been performing.

Warner and its archrival Columbia Records, owned by CBS, are in the midst of a fierce battle in 1978. In 1977, James Taylor had left Warner for Columbia and released *JT,* a huge hit. Warner, meanwhile, had signed Paul Simon away from Columbia after the singer-songwriter had made six albums for that label. Bonnie Raitt, another up-and-coming singer-guitarist on the Warner label, had gotten a large offer from Columbia that Warner was forced to match lest it lose yet another star.

In a preview of the label's brief relationship with Tommy Tutone, Warner had chosen to "mainstream" Raitt's sound, eliminating many of her famous guitar licks in favor of more pop-oriented vocals. About the album *Takin My Time,* one reviewer complained "of an overly slick record that downplays Bonnie's gutsy qualities as singer and sacrifices feeling for mechanical precision."

Nevertheless, Tommy and Jim enter the studio and begin recording many of the tracks that will appear on their first album, although they still lack a formal recording contract. They also hire Brian Rohan, one of the most powerful entertainment lawyers in the Bay Area. Rohan, a formidable negotiator who had secured lucrative recording contracts for hit groups including the Cars and Boston, will deal with the labels, letting Tommy and Jim concentrate on their music. As recording for the demo begins, negotiations with Warner for a multi-album deal take off. And go nowhere.

Rohan has enough industry pull to prevent the label from securing publishing rights from Tommy and Jim, a key victory for the musicians. But Rohan and Warner will battle for months over other contract terms, and of course over money. Meanwhile, other labels, sensing blood in the water, begin nosing around, trying to determine if Warner is serious about signing the band. At one point, an offer even comes in from ARC Records, the label created by Maurice White, of the seventies supergroup Earth, Wind & Fire. Columbia, too, has heard about Tommy Tutone and is anxious to determine the status of the Warner discussions.

In the studio, meanwhile, Tommy and Jim are having difficulties. ("We couldn't agree on anything," Tommy recalls years later.) Though Tommy is the leader onstage, most of the band's songs are written by Jim or his songwriting partners. In the recording studio, neither has a clearly defined role, and as a result tensions rise. Decisions on songs, and arrangements, are protracted and painful. After several months of work, "Rachel," "Am I Supposed to Lie," "Sounds of a Summer Night," and several of the band's other early tracks, including "Angel Say No," one of Jim's best songwriting efforts, are laid down.

Finally, at the end of 1978, negotiations with Warner come to a head. Attorney Rohan gives an ultimatum: Make a reasonable offer within thirty days or the band walks—and offers the demos to other interested parties. Warner backs away, and Columbia, in the form of Terry Powell, steps in.

Rohan had sent the demo tape to Powell, Columbia's manager of West Coast A & R and an eighteen-year veteran of the company. Powell has worked with scores of successful artists, among them Toto, Neil Diamond, Chicago, and Pink Floyd, and is determined to get Tommy Tutone. "I loved that tape," Powell later recalls. "I thought Tommy sounded a lot like Van Morrison." He flies up to the Northern California town of Willets to hear Tommy Tutone; the band is playing in a bowling alley.

After learning that the group has no management, Terry sets up a gig for potential managers to hear and meet them. Among those invited is Paul Cheslaw. Cheslaw is based in Los Angeles and has worked successfully with George Harrison, Santana, and the promoter Bill Graham, among many others; he travels to San Francisco to meet Tommy and Jim. "I remember coming backstage at a club just as Tony Dimitriades, who managed Tom Petty, was leaving," Cheslaw recalls years later. "And there were two other managers being introduced by their attorney, Brian Rohan. In the end, I became their manager."

Within a month Terry offers the group a Columbia recording contract. The "pub-rock" band, formed less than a year before, has a record label, and a three-album deal.

❋

In early 1979, Tommy and Jim, along with the bassist Terry Nails and the drummer Micky Shine, enter the studio and begin laying down tracks for *Tommy Tutone,* their first album. But even before the record is complete, songs are leaking out and getting lots of attention. One in particular, "Cheap Date," a quirky reggae-inspired track, is bootlegged and has "somehow" found its way onto radio station playlists. In fact the leak, and the band's subsequent "anger" about it, was a publicity scheme cooked up by Cheslaw and Columbia in order to garner media attention and make the band seem more "antiestablishment." "We had a lot of creative ideas," recalls Paul Cheslaw, clearly enjoying the memory of that exciting period. "We purposely printed the press release and bio in a format that looked like it was done on the cheap by a new, struggling band (cheap printing, no evidence of the Columbia press machine, New Wave graphics) to appeal to the 'New Wave' movement."

Paul also realizes that Columbia is so busy promoting its more established acts that, without help, Tommy Tutone is going to fade away, like so many other bands that have come before. "It was apparent that the record company [had] to prioritize its promotional spending and would only respond once radio started to notice the record," he recalls. A core team of Tommy Tutone believers, including Paul, Terry, and the Columbia promoters Mike Gussler, Ron Oberman, and David Gales, get behind the band. The group, also friends, hires a number of independent promoters who have established relationships with disc jockeys and station list managers. These people convince the stations to play the Tommy Tutone album.

One of the people Paul will eventually hire is an independent promoter named Jon Scott, and Scott comes through at once, getting the band the airplay that will force their label to spend the critical promotional dollars. "Jon truly masterminded the game and delivered the results," Paul says later.

The results are remarkable. By the time the album's first true single, "Angel Say No," is released in early 1980, Tommy Tutone is generating the buzz so critical to success in the music business. "Angel Say No" charts in the *Billboard* magazine Top 40 in the spring, propelling the album to respectable sales, more than 100,000 by the end of the year. Soon other, bigger bands come calling. Jon Scott approaches the band with a compelling offer: Would Tommy Tutone consider opening for Tom Petty and the Heartbreakers on their 1980 tour?

Scott, Tommy knows, is a talented and well-connected music promoter. Scott had first seen Petty in Los Angeles in the mid-seventies, after the band moved to the West Coast from Gainesville. At the time the Heartbreakers were opening for Blondie, playing a two-week run of shows at the Whisky in Hollywood, and also performing at the Starwood. "I remember this one fellow, Jon Scott, walking up to me out of the blue and saying, 'You don't know me, but you're going to know me because I'm going to get your record "Breakdown" played on the radio,' " Petty later recalls. "And he did."

Petty's first two albums, 1976's *Tom Petty and the Heartbreakers* and 1978's *You're Gonna Get It!* had sold modestly. But after successful gigs in Europe, the band had found their audience and, with Scott's help, their 1979 album, *Damn the Torpedoes,* sold millions, making Petty a star. Tommy and Jim jump at the opportunity to open for Petty, and are soon playing to arena crowds numbering in the thousands. "I remember I stood on the side of the stage every night, watching Petty," Jim later says. "It was something so exciting to see, an incredible time."

But there are also some ominous signs, indications that their first album is less than a smash hit. Columbia decides to release two more singles from *Tommy Tutone,* "Cheap Date" and "Girl in the Back Seat," hoping they will ride the success of "Angel" and move more records. Neither song charts, though, and soon "Angel" itself has fallen from regular rotation. Tommy and Jim are also at odds, unable to write music together, with anger about who will get credit for songs simmering just below the surface. By early 1981, sales for the album begin trailing off.

But in that year, one of the most important in the history of contemporary music, a piece of incredible luck will arrive, setting the stage for the success of "Jenny." It comes in the form of a small cable television station that will go on to revolutionize popular culture. The station is called MTV: The Music Channel.

❁

In the spring of 1981, executives at Warner Amex Satellite Entertainment were basking in the glow of their successful cable channel aimed at youngsters, called Nickelodeon, which had been launched in 1979. But they were looking for another cable hit.

Warner Amex, as the company was known, was a joint venture of Warner Communications and American Express, led by senior vice president Bob Pittman. (Pittman would later head America Online, after that company's purchase of Time Warner, before being ousted in 2002.) Pittman was in search of programming that would appeal to teens, and company officials proposed a music-oriented channel that would allow record companies to showcase their talent to the music-buying generation. (A similar concept, in the form of a show called *Video Jukebox,* aired occasionally on the pay-cable network Home Box Office.)

In addition to its twenty-four hours of music programming per day, the channel would have several other innovative features. It would be the first TV channel broadcast in stereo. It would be the first created by the company to accept advertising. It would also be provided free to cable operators, and thus to viewers. And, as an added incentive, Warner Amex would make available two of the eight minutes of advertising each hour to the cable operators for their own use.

The goal, according to Robert McGroarty, senior vice president for marketing and sales, was to sign up cable companies with a total of 1.5 million subscribers by the airdate, set for August 1, 1981. By the end of June, more than 2 million households had signed on. By the end of July, the number had grown to 2.5 million. Early advertisers included soft drink, beer, and entertainment companies.

In what was perhaps one of the greatest programming coups in modern television history, Warner Amex had also devised a novel way to provide its content at minimal cost to the company: It would let the record companies spend their own money to create the video "promos" that MTV would air—a strategy still in use today (though of course MTV now has its own programs as well). MTV would, essentially, give record companies unlimited time to broadcast what were in essence glorified commercials for their products. And record companies scrambled to pay for the privilege.

But another aspect of the new channel would prove even more important, and incredibly lucky, for Tommy Tutone. Because in the early 1980s few U.S. record labels had major video production facilities, MTV was forced to rely on imports, specifically British New Wave videos, which were popular on television in the United Kingdom.

The commercial success of New Wave music from 1979 to 1983 would correspond almost exactly with MTV's rise. Elvis Costello, widely considered the first commercially successful New Wave artist, was the first musician of the genre to chart in the United States, making it onto the *Billboard* Top 100 album list in 1978. By 1982, 23 percent of new artists in the *Billboard* Top 100 albums and 27 percent of new artists in the Top 100 singles were New Wave.

❖

After a successful tour with the Heartbreakers, and based on sales of the first album and "Angel Say No," Columbia asks Tommy and Jim to return to the studio for a second album.

Songwriting and recording for the album, to be called *Tommy Tutone–2,* progress slowly. By early 1981 the band has recorded a full album's worth of material, only to be told by the label that they need more (and, obviously, better) tracks. Jim once again collaborates with the songwriter Alex Call, of the seventies band Clover, which had disbanded in 1978. (Micky Shine had also played with Clover, although two other Clover band members, Huey Lewis and Sean Hopper, would go on to find fame as Huey Lewis and the News.)

During the recording sessions for the second round of songs, Jim approaches Tommy with a song called "Jenny," which, he and Alex feel, has real potential. The lyrics tell the story of a somewhat disturbed guy who sees some scrawl on a bathroom wall. Under the name "Jenny" and the words "For a good time call . . ." a phone number, "867-5309," is given. The first verse and bridge, Tommy sees, are catchy:

Jenny Jenny who can I turn to
You give me something I can hold on to
I know you'll think I'm like the others before
Who saw your name and number on the wall

Jenny I've got your number
I need to make you mine
Jenny don't change your number

The music starts with a guitar fading in from silence, builds to a crescendo, then continues behind the lyric with a great hook that's perfect for the band. A compact 3:44, the song is also perfect for radio, Tommy knows. The strange chorus, nothing but a phone number, features a cool call and response section:

Eight six seven five three oh niii-yine (Tommy)
Eight six seven five three oh niii-yine (band)
Eight six seven five three oh niii-yine (Tommy)
Eight six seven five three oh niii-yine (band)

Though the song describes a lonely, desperate kid who knows that "for the price of a dime I can always turn to you," the real Jenny story is somewhat more prosaic. Jim and Alex had been working on song arrangements in a rented cargo container near the Marin County dump, which Alex used as a cheap studio. "Jenny" was simply the re-sult of a particularly successful recording session. "We were not the first songwriters to write a song about a phone number," Jim says later. "Wilson Pickett had a song called '634-5789,' which probably influenced us, if unconsciously."

When Jim later gave an interview telling the decidedly unglam-orous tale behind the song, Columbia immediately told him to make up a more interesting story, and the Jenny legend was born: The number, the story went, belonged to a particularly cute girl who had once operated the sound board at a club in Carmel, California.

The band works on the arrangement for a few days, and even-tually the song, officially titled "867-5309/Jenny," makes it to the album's final cut. Tommy and Jim have been in the studio for a year.

With the help of Mark Robinson, a producer in Venice, Califor-nia, the band also records a promotional video for "Jenny," as well as one for "Which Man Are You," another song from the album. Like many videos of the time, the "Jenny" video cuts from a "live perfor-mance" (actually studio footage made to appear live) to filmed action sequences that offer a more narrative version of the subject of the song.

But the "Jenny" video goes further, adding a twist to the story. "We were one of the first bands to figure out that, to make a good video, you needed a story that was more than just the story of the song," Tommy later recalls. In the video, a beautiful blond woman in a bar hands Tommy her name and phone number scribbled on a piece of paper. Afraid to call her, he becomes obsessed, following her and peeking into her window while she undresses. He goes to see a therapist (played by Jim Keller), who also seems to become fixated on Jenny, repeating her phone number, "867-5309," during their sessions. Finally, while peeking through her window, Tommy sees Jenny kissing another man. As he is led off by the police, he sees that the other man is his therapist, a sly Jim Keller. The video ends with a police mug shot of Tommy, prisoner number 8675309.

A fortuitous connection helps get the video to MTV's attention. Hearing that the new station was on the verge of beginning its broadcast life, Columbia had brought on a small team of publicity people to create promotions specifically for television. "A young woman had just started a new role within the record company creating videos and liaising with MTV," Paul Cheslaw later recalls. "MTV at the time needed content, and [we] thought 'Jenny' would be perfect for that summer teen audience. We put together creative promotional events around 'Jenny' that ensured that MTV played it."

Tommy Tutone–2 is scheduled for release in December 1981. The album's first single, "867-5309/Jenny," and the song's video are ready to go by the fall. On August 1, 1981, a switch is flipped at Warner Amex Satellite Entertainment. At a minute past midnight, MTV is born, and "Video Killed the Radio Star," by the Buggles, is on television.

○

The "Jenny" video is picked up by MTV almost immediately, and is played relentlessly for the first few months of the station's existence. "In the early 1980s, middle America was just not being served by the music industry, which was all Top 40 at that time," recalls Alan Hunter, in 1981 a member of the first group of MTV video jockeys, or "VJs." "Then all of a sudden you have these New Wave and pop bands that come along and sing about a guy and his girl, about you and your baby, and they had this instant appeal," Hunter says. He adds that what "Jenny" and videos like it brought to the fore was a new vision of what music videos could be. "The earliest videos, from the late seventies, told a very linear story. But this quickly changed to a less literal, more surreal style. Tommy Tutone's video was one of the earliest to offer a conceptualized version of the song."

While by today's standards the MTV audience in 1981 was limited, the station reached a million viewers. Though when it began life MTV was not broadcast in Los Angeles or New York, in Middle America it immediately became a powerful force in the music industry. "It was just amazing. I remember being recognized on the street in places like Iowa," Jim recalls. "Kids would say, 'Look, there goes the psychiatrist!' "

Many musicians, including the at the time ubiquitous Billy Idol, credited MTV with changing the way radio station program directors picked music. "Once the people out there, the kids or whoever it is, saw the videos, liked the music, then they phoned up the radio people and forced those local stations to play your music," Idol said. "It set the stage for a lot of what's happened in American music since," he added. Idol believes that MTV was able to break the historic grip that radio had on the music industry.

The fortuitous confluence of song and fledgling video channel has an immediate impact. With the "Jenny" video in constant rotation and the song all over the radio, *Tommy Tutone–2* builds in popularity. By late in 1981 "Jenny" has charted. The song soon peaks in the top 5, coming in at number 4 on the *Billboard* chart in January 1982.

Several clever publicity schemes conceived by Paul Cheslaw and Columbia keep the video on the air and create huge headaches for people unlucky enough to own an "867-5309" phone number. "We got national press attention when we promoted the fact that people across the country with 867-5309 were having to change their numbers, a change the record company was paying for," Cheslaw remembers. *People* magazine even picks up the story, and in a three-page spread includes Cheslaw's phone number, encouraging people with complaints to call him. "What I got," Cheslaw recalls, "was a visit from phone company management complaining about the overload problems, which generated additional coverage."

The single soon goes gold, signifying sales of half a million copies, and Tommy Tutone is suddenly a hot commodity. The album rides the song's coattails, reaching number 20 in the spring.

The summer of 1982 is a great one for the band. Touring with acts like Cheap Trick and ZZ Top, Tommy Tutone plays to packed arenas and finally begins to see some money. "I had a credit card for the first time in my life, and an accountant to pay my bills," Jim remembers. Based on "Jenny" 's massive radio airplay, the music publishing company BMI advances the band fifty thousand dollars in performance royalties. Tommy and Jim are even asked to pen a song for the 1982 soft-core movie *The Last American Virgin*. They write "Teen Angel Eyes" in "about 10 minutes" for twenty thousand dollars.

But by September, things begin to change. "Jenny," which rose so fast, plummets with equal speed. ("When they fall, they fall fast," Tommy observes ruefully.) The "Jenny" video soon falls out of MTV's rotation. Columbia pushes "Which Man Are You" as the album's second single. The song, while less than three minutes long, is a more deliberate track that lacks a good guitar hook; the slower beat also makes it virtually undanceable. It fails to chart. (Tommy believes Columbia should have pushed "Baby It's Alright," a rollicking song with a great beat, as the second single. And, indeed, the album has lots of good material, including the pulsing "Shadow on the Road Ahead," an excellent "car" song reminiscent of Jackson Browne's best. In this context, Columbia's choice is inexplicable.)

Still, there are rays of hope. Based on the amazing success of "Jenny" and their second album, Tommy and Jim enter the studio in late 1982 for a third album. The all-critical follow-up to a smash hit is a chance to keep the momentum going.

Unfortunately, things begin falling apart in all directions. Once the group achieved success with *Tommy Tutone–2,* their manager, Paul Cheslaw, says, "the wolves started sniffing around." The band is approached by Frontline, a powerful management company in Los Angeles with a stable of successful recording acts, including the Eagles and Stevie Nicks. Frontline makes a tempting offer for a young band: If they come onboard, Frontline will, based on the success of "Jenny," aggressively renegotiate their contract, securing a much more lucrative deal for their third album. (Tommy and Jim recall that Paul had other acts to manage and was disorganized at the time, and the band was looking for someone with more focus.)

After several meetings with various attorneys and with and without band members, Frontline offers Paul the opportunity to come on the team as well, bringing his other acts into the fold. "I was not comfortable with their strategy, and I decided not to join Frontline," he recalls. "At that point the band had a choice: Go with Frontline or stay with me." Paul knows that Jim is leaning toward Frontline. But for Tommy, he feels sure, the music, and their relationship, is the most important thing.

"Tommy and Jim did not have the same perspective on how important Tommy Tutone was," Paul says. "For Tommy, this was a career; he was always going to be Tommy Tutone. Being a musician was his life. For Jim, this was a youthful pastime, and he always knew that he was going to do something else when he 'grew up.' " Jim agrees. "There are some guys that are lifers, but I had other interests; I knew there were other things I could do. I wasn't going to go down in a blaze of cigarette butts and empty beer cans, playing in a bar somewhere when I was in my sixties."

Paul is disappointed when Tommy also arrives at the decision to go with Frontline. "I felt pretty hurt by Tommy going along with that scenario," he remembers. Eventually an agreement is arranged that will give Paul some continuing compensation, based on the success of the third album. In late 1982 the band and their manager part company.

It is a decision that will prove costly.

◉

The third record becomes an albatross. Musically, Tommy and Jim try too hard to produce a "concept album," looking to make a statement as well as a record. "Everyone used to tell us, 'You're great because you're so sparse,' " Tommy later recalls. "We said, 'Fuck that, we'll make a wall-of-sound album instead.' " Both Tommy and Jim have moved to Los Angeles, away from their musical roots, and neither feels grounded. "It just became too much about the business, and not about the music," Jim adds. Recording drags on, month after month, and neither man is happy with the chosen material.

Meanwhile, things at Columbia are changing, too, and not for the better. In 1979 the record industry had been shocked by falling sales. As one observer later noted, for an industry accustomed to uninterrupted yearly profit increases since the 1950s, this was not simply a dip: It was a disaster. With the economy in recession, in June

1982 the CBS Records division had laid off nearly three hundred people. Terry Powell, the band's main advocate at the label (who remains Tommy's friend) was let go. "The company had a new president, and he hated my guts," Powell later recalls. "But he didn't last long either." In October, CBS closed its record manufacturing plant in Terre Haute, Indiana, and consolidated several other vinyl production facilities. Thousands lost their jobs.

In fact CBS Records, at the time still the largest record company in the world, was getting ready for major shifts in the recording industry. Independent labels and distributors were disappearing, being bought up by the majors. By the mid-1980s, the six major labels (Warner, CBS, RCA, MCA, Capitol-EMI, and Polygram) would control the distribution of virtually all recorded music produced in the United States. (In the 1990s, the number of companies would shrink to four and would manufacture or distribute four-fifths of all artists on the pop charts.) In 1982, CBS and Sony had created a jointly owned manufacturing facility for the newest recording technology, compact discs. In 1983 Sony would buy out CBS's stake. A few years later Sony would buy CBS Records outright, for $2 billion.

Things at MTV are different as well. By 1983 the music video channel has tripled its audience (to almost 7 million viewers) and is on its way to 16 million viewers, and profitability. But the channel soon finds that success brings its own problems. For the first time, officials begin to see a backlash against MTV's growing power in the recording industry, particularly from African-American musicians who cannot get their music on the shows. "One outlet like MTV can be more far-reaching than a number of radio stations," said George Ware, executive director of the Black Music Association. "They are the only game in town," added Solomon Roberts, Jr., a member of the rhythm and blues group Sky. (Only in the mid-1980s, with the rise of artists like Michael Jackson and Run-D.M.C., will MTV begin regular rotation of music videos by African-American artists.)

MTV's increasing leverage is apparent at the retail level, too. A *Billboard* survey in late 1982 found that record sales rose 15 to 20 percent after exposure on MTV. Terry Powell later recalls that "MTV was just explosive in the industry. You could immediately tell the impact in the market when a record went on the air." But sadly, for many artists the opposite was also true, and remains true today: Without music video exposure, it is almost impossible to sell music. "The industry has changed," laments Powell. "Today it's brutal, all red and black. I always felt you had to develop an artist and stick with them. Now, if you don't have a hit today, you're history."

❖

After more than a year in the studio, late in 1983 the band's third—and final—album, *National Emotion,* is released. The record's liner notes are perhaps a telling reflection of the turmoil in the band: Nearly twenty musicians, engineers, and producers are credited. ("We even had Toto on that record," Jim later recalls.) With no one in the company acting as an advocate for the band, Columbia fails to promote the album, and no singles chart. One reviewer sums it up succinctly: "Nothing could follow up '867-5309/Jenny,' and it seems the band realized that. *National Emotion* finds the band going through the motions, half-heartedly repeating the formula of *Tommy Tutone–2,* rocking harder in places but generally lacking inspiration."

The production delays on *National Emotion* had proved costly. By 1983, when 43 percent and 50 percent, respectively, of new artists on the albums and singles charts were New Wave, the style had peaked. Nineteen eighty-four would see a precipitous drop in New Wave's popularity, with the same percentages falling to 22 and 27.

None of the songs from *National Emotion* appear on MTV.

There was more to the failure of the third Tommy Tutone album, however, than shifts in music tastes and recording industry cutbacks. In a business where relationships can make or break careers, Tommy and Jim had, in the eyes of some, forgotten about the people who had contributed to their rise. "Tommy and Jim never realized just how much their success was created by a team larger than themselves, and that they were not at the stage where they had built a career yet," their former manager Paul Cheslaw recalls. "Relationships are very important in the music business. They contribute to the network that surrounds all successful performers. The problem for artists is that news travels fast, and those [who] build you up can tear you down very quickly."

Some contend that Columbia's decision not to promote *National Emotion* was less structural than personal. When word got out that Tommy Tutone had moved to Frontline, people were angry, Paul Cheslaw remembers. "Once they changed management, there were people in the record company who wanted to teach them a lesson, [and] once Terry was gone [the band] had no one on their side after they tried to renegotiate their contract," Paul says. "One critical Columbia executive in financial affairs made the direct comment 'We'll show them.' " Jim Keller has no doubt that Frontline went in to Columbia and tried to dictate terms, and Tommy Tutone paid the price for such hubris.

The year 1983 proved to be the end of the line for Tommy Tutone the band. After selling more than half a million copies of "Jenny" and several hundred thousand albums, and making millions for their record company, Tommy and Jim left Columbia. "They were just starting to walk but [felt] that they were ready to run," says Paul Cheslaw. "They paid an expensive price when they fell." Unable to find another label, Tommy and Jim went their separate ways. Tommy later said, "We could no longer agree, and it seemed like the time had passed, so we called it quits."

Jim would drift in and out of music for several years, playing in bands, writing commercial jingles, and eventually using his knowledge of the business to oversee Philip Glass's music publishing company in New York City. Tommy would move to Nashville to try writing country music, then in 1996 to the Portland, Oregon, area to become a software engineer. Terry Powell would go on to form a small independent music company, which he later sold to European investors. Paul Cheslaw, disillusioned with musicians and the music business, moved into the technology industry. He later became a management consultant and also works on sustainable development projects in South Africa, Madagascar, and Mozambique. Of the group, only Tommy and Terry have kept in touch. For the others, their "weak ties" were severed, along with the band, in 1983.

In the years since "Jenny," Tommy has continued to write and play music, and has released a number of albums to critical acclaim (though not commercial success). Nineteen ninety-six brought *Nervous Love,* which one critic hailed as "a fine collection of mainly working-class/bar-band rock and roll crossed with power-pop that isn't too dissimilar to Tommy Tutone's heyday." In 1998 Tommy released *tutone.rtf,* of which a reviewer wrote the following:

Yes, it's that Tommy Tutone. If you're not that old, "Jenny (867-5309)" might ring a bell. No matter what comes after 1981, he'll always be forever linked to that name and number, which is a real shame with such a fine release. . . . [It's] unfortunate that artists like Tommy have such a stigma attached to their name.

Now in a new band, Tommy Tutone also tours occasionally with, among other acts, the Knack.

❀

Many musicians deserve their one-hit wonder status, mostly because they had minimal talent to begin with. The group Milli Vanilli, who lip-synched their way through a series of hit songs, immediately comes to mind (and they sold 30 million records). Other bands, however, have the songwriting skills, the vocal range, and the musical chops to succeed but never make it beyond a single song. These groups are forever relegated—no matter how undeservedly—to one-hit wonder status.

Is their fate simply the luck of the draw? Perhaps, and of course life isn't fair. But for better or worse, in the music industry both good and bad luck are highly dependent on the whim of record labels. Good luck with one label (Tommy Tutone's move from Warner to Columbia, and hooking up with Terry Powell and Paul Cheslaw) can become bad luck (Columbia's abandonment of the band) when management shake-ups take place or relationships are severed. And, now more than ever, MTV can make or break the luck of any band with a simple programming decision. It is the rare band that succeeds on talent alone.

The series of relationships Tommy and Jim had—a few lasting, most not—played a major role in positioning them for the success of "Jenny." But of course those same relationships contributed to their demise, as personnel, organizational, and cultural changes in the band, at their label, and at MTV brought an end to the group, and eventually to New Wave altogether.

How does Tommy view his luck? Does he feel lucky, or unlucky? "I saw so many bands do worse," he says. "I saw forty bands signed to CBS. Twenty of them made albums, and two of them got promoted, and I was one of them. So I was very lucky in that sense."

In the end, Tommy and Jim seem to have cultivated the healthiest attitude toward their luck, both good and bad. Dealing with being tagged a one-hit wonder is all a matter of perspective. Yes, having only one hit in a musical career is clearly a difficult thing. But, Tommy says, it's better than no hit at all.

"There were really some great parts, being in a band, having a hit song," Jim says nostalgically. "You know, you start when you're just a kid, playing in a bar, and it's all so much fun. Then you grow up, and you watch these shows on MTV and VH1 about one-hit wonders, and the segment always ends with the person saying the same thing: 'I'm working on a new record, and it's the best thing I've ever done.' Well, you know what?" he continues. "You're not supposed to hold on to it. That was about being twenty-five and about that moment. And it was amazing. But it was that moment."

Does he regret being a one-hit wonder? "How can I?" Jim says. "That's like saying I regret my youth."

CHAPTER 5

We Have Lost Both Engines

Amy Knowlton isn't thinking about dying, at least not yet. She isn't thinking about her family either, or about God, or about the raft. Instead, she's thinking about Brian Hoover's bare feet and poor Rachel Bedelsky, who is still throwing up in the front seat.

She's also doing two things at once: bracing for impact and yelling, "Mayday! Mayday!" into her small, handheld marine radio, hoping that someone on the other end can hear her. She's also listening to George Masson on his radio, trying to tell someone their position. Without a Loran, she knows, neither of them can give the precise coordinates of their location. Instead, they can give only approximations: bearing, flying time, and speed. But is this enough information for someone to find them?

As she prepares for impact, she continues to yell: "Mayday, Mayday! We have lost both engines! Repeat, we have lost both engines!

We are going to ditch. Repeat, we are going to ditch!" No response. In seconds, they hit the ocean. Seconds later, still strapped to her seat, Amy feels water up to her knees. They are sinking, she quickly realizes, and the water is freezing.

It is then that she remembers her radio isn't waterproof.

◉

The word *luck* is often associated with accidents, particularly plane crashes. A passenger on a plane that crashes is considered "unlucky," while a survivor is thought of as "lucky to be alive." Luck plays a role in air disasters because plane crashes are unpredictable (or their causes are hidden at the time), and the odds against them are high. Flying is not inherently risky, however, and people who fly accept the trade-off of a tiny amount of risk for the convenience offered by air travel.

But what is the relationship between luck and risk? Do we invite bad luck when we take risks? And if so, what steps should we take to counter the possible unlucky outcomes of risky behavior? Clearly those who take risks unnecessarily open themselves up to bad luck. But a moderate amount of risk taking is a part of life, and some risks—crossing the street, driving a car—cannot easily be avoided. One key, it seems, is effective risk assessment. We may not always know the odds, but we can do our best to limit our risks: "The sagacious person avoids unnecessary and excessive risks," says the philosopher Nicholas Rescher, "keeping the odds in her favor so as to minimize the extent to which reliance need be placed on luck to save the day."

Another, related aspect of good risk assessment is preparation. We can be in a position to overcome bad luck (or capitalize on good luck) by taking precautions and making the proper preparations whenever possible. Of course, without good information, effective planning isn't always an option, and most risk assessment naturally occurs in conditions of uncertainty. And, further, when risks are shared among interdependent people, the actions of one person can affect the choices available to the others. As Amy and her group would discover, choices made by their pilot severely limited their ability to plan for an accident.

But that does not mean her preparation was wasted. Once her bad-luck event occurred, much of Amy's immediate fate was in the hands of the pilot, Masson. But her earlier decision to bring her marine radio probably saved her life, and the lives of the other passengers. That decision, based more on emotional factors than on a purely cognitive assessment of the risks involved in the flight, luckily turned out to be the right one. But there is also evidence that people who use their emotions when they assess risks are more likely to find success in subsequent tasks.

Behavioral evidence suggests that risk preference is often determined by emotion, one study has found. Further, researchers argue, emotional reactions guide responses not only at their first occurrence but also through conditioning and memory later, which can serve as somatic markers. People who lack these markers "not only have difficulty making risky decisions, but they also choose in ways that turn their personal and professional lives to shambles."

Using her emotions and her instincts, Amy also provided an opening for the piece of good luck, in the form of an off-duty radio operator, that would save her life.

❀

As she prepares to board the small Cessna Skymaster 337, Amy Knowlton feels a chill in the air. Even for northern Florida, which is by no means tropical, today is overcast and cold, probably in the fifties, she guesses. It is 9:30 A.M. on Monday, January 26, 1987, and she and four colleagues, along with their volunteer pilot, are at the Fernandina Beach Municipal Airport, on Amelia Island, Florida, preparing for takeoff. They are a mixed bag, this group, though all share an interest in marine biology, whales in particular.

The three other researchers, Rachel, Brian, and Scott Mercer, are all paid seasonals, basically temp workers out of Boston, hired by the New England Aquarium for a few months of monitoring right whale migration patterns. Right whales are so named because, as far back as the 1100s, they were known to be the "right whales" to kill. Growing to sixty feet in length, the huge animals have an unusually thick blubber layer and float easily once dead, making them ideal targets for whalers. Once with an enormous population, they had been hunted virtually to extinction in the North Atlantic well into the nineteenth century; by 1970, only a small remnant population remained.

Because of their small numbers, very little was known about right whale breeding and migratory patterns until, in 1979, several whales were spotted by Dave Mattingly, a pilot for Delta Air Lines. Recruiting some fellow airmen to volunteer their private planes and their time, the pilot and his colleagues began to survey the roving whale population. In 1984 a breakthrough occurred: The same mother-calf pair was spotted near the coast of northern Florida in the winter and then in the Bay of Fundy, off Nova Scotia, in the summer. It appeared that the whales migrated to the southern Atlantic to calve, then swam all the way back to the cold waters off Canada when the birthing was complete. The coastal area off the Georgia-Florida border, it turned out, was the only known calving ground for the species. Later that year, Mattingly and Scott Kraus of the New England Aquarium began the first dedicated right whale surveys in the country.

Amy had begun working at the New England Aquarium in 1983, after receiving a B.A. in geography from Boston University. Having spent a semester at sea while in school, she felt that the aquarium was the perfect place for someone with her mapmaking and boat-handling skills—and it allowed her to be near the sea, a big plus. When she was offered the chance to try to spot some of the elusive whales in Florida, she jumped at it.

Except there were no whales, or so it seemed. Although they had completed several flights since their work began a few weeks before, the group had yet to see a single whale. Indeed, they had seen almost nothing at all, or at least nothing aside from long expanses of dark ocean, and the occasional freighter plowing through it.

As a result, Amy and the others have decided to expand their search area, hoping that the deeper waters farther from the coast might yield at least a few whale sightings. Amy looks at her clipboard, filled with sheets denoting their prospective search grids. She again notes that today, for the first time, they will follow a search pattern that will take them many miles out, beyond even the entrance to the Savannah shipping channel.

Their twin-engine Cessna Skymaster 337 is sometimes called a "push-pull" because of its odd-looking in-line engine configuration: one prop in front of the cabin, one behind it. It is a reliable plane but also an old one: A modified version of the same plane had been used during the war in Vietnam. Their particular aircraft, which had been lent to them by an Amelia Island resident, dates from the sixties, though it seems to be in good overall condition.

While the pilot was fairly familiar with the aircraft and its controls, he knew the plane had several quirks that made it less than ideal for a nearly full-day flight over open water. Masson had informed the group that they would follow a simple search pattern, flying forty miles east, then south three miles, west forty miles, and north and back east again. However, because the aircraft had no Loran receiver—a powerful radio navigation device that determines exact latitude and longitude—they would use a compass, in conjunction with their distance and airspeed, to roughly calculate their location. They would fly at about 750 feet, a relatively low altitude, but one that would allow them to spot whales in the area.

The Skymaster's history, like its looks, is something of an oddity. At the end of World War II, the Cessna Aircraft Company had found—and appropriated, as war reparations—an experimental Luftwaffe airplane created by Dornier, a respected German aircraft designer. The strange-looking plane with its fore-aft engine configuration had been tested and rejected by the Germans because of, among other things, the difficulty in reliably getting fuel to the two engines. (One observer noted that Cessna "took the plane but forgot the test data.") Other choices made by Cessna, including the design of the auxiliary fuel tanks in the wings, made the plane susceptible to potentially catastrophic hazards, including air and debris in the fuel lines. This and several additional fuel flow problems had been addressed by a number of FAA Airworthiness Directives dating back to 1970.

For a small plane, the Skymaster has a highly complex fuel system that could stymie pilots unaccustomed to the aircraft's quirks. The plane has four fuel tanks—one main tank and one auxiliary tank in each wing. Tanks in the left wing typically feed the front engine, while those in the right feed the rear. There is also a cross-connect capability, which allows the right main tank to feed the front engine and the left main to feed the rear.

Each engine has a fuel selector switch, which determines how fuel is fed to the fuel injection system. For example, the front engine selector switch can be set to allow fuel to flow from the left main, left auxiliary, or right main, but not from the right auxiliary, tank. The situation is reversed for the rear engine: fuel can come only from the right main, the right aux, or the left main. The selector switches are also highly sensitive: If they are not seated exactly in the proper position, the pilot may think that he has switched tanks when in fact he has not.

Another odd aspect of the system's design is that the fuel flowing into an engine is roughly twice the amount the engine uses; excess fuel and vapor are always returned to that engine's principal tank, regardless of the tank the mixture came from. These characteristics have a number of serious implications for flying time. The first is that while the auxiliary tanks hold eighteen gallons each, or theoretically about two hours of flying time, in fact, since double the necessary amount of fuel is flowing to the engines, the tanks run dry after about an hour. Even more worrisome, if the excess fuel that is returned to the main tanks finds those tanks already full, that excess has no place to go and is vented overboard, shortening the flight time of the aircraft even further. A pilot without the benefit of this knowledge might find himself in a difficult situation if his tanks began to run dry.

While this strange system was common to virtually all Skymaster 337s, this group's particular aircraft had its own mechanical problems. Amy knew that their plane had reported a disturbing incident a few days before. Their pilot had been flying with Dr. Phillip Tedrick, the owner of the plane, and some problem—still undiagnosed—had developed when the fuel flow was switched between the auxiliary and the main tanks. The switch had caused one of the engines to fail. The pilot had been able to restart it after some tense moments, and the flight had otherwise been uneventful. While she found this a bit unusual, Amy was not especially concerned. She knew the plane could stay aloft with only one functional engine.

Pilots of the Cessna Skymaster are taught not to rely on the aircraft's fuel gauges, which are notoriously unreliable (as they are on many small aircraft). Masson's flight plan was to take off using his main tanks, fly for a few hours on the auxiliary tanks, then switch back over to the mains for the remainder of the flight and landing. In this way he would not have to rely on his fuel gauges, since he knew he would have plenty of fuel left in the main tanks when the auxiliary tanks began to run dry. It seemed a sensible precaution to everyone. And besides, Masson explained, along with their life jackets, on this flight they would be bringing a small inflatable life raft. Just in case.

On most small planes, where the order in which the tanks are used is immaterial, Masson's plan would have worked perfectly. But because of the peculiar design of the Skymaster, it would prove disastrous.

✦

Amy puts her camera equipment aboard, pulling her wool sweater tighter against the morning chill. The sky is a mass of dull gray cloud, overcast as far as the horizon. She takes her seat, directly behind the pilot, noticing that Brian, as usual, has taken off his sneakers. For some reason, she knows, he likes to fly barefoot. She fastens her seat belt, then checks her marine radio to make sure it's working properly. She's taken it primarily because it allows her to communicate with ships below, giving her the opportunity to ask them about any possible whale sightings in the area. But it also gives them a direct way to contact the Coast Guard. Just in case.

The plane taxies slowly, picks up speed down the runway, and then is airborne, turning due east and heading out over the cold waters of the Atlantic.

❖

The first two hours of the flight pass without incident, and without any whale sightings. While most of the group is comfortable, if slightly bored, Rachel, in the copilot's seat, is in bad shape. Prone to airsickness, she is vomiting, seemingly without pause, into a small container in her lap. Sympathetic, yet slightly annoyed, the others do their best to ignore the sound—and the smell.

After flying several legs of the search pattern, pilot Masson calculates that the fuel in the reserve tanks is probably running low. He reaches above his head, turning the selector switch for the rear engine, which will alter the fuel flow from the auxiliary to the main tank. The changeover appears to have occurred without incident. They are more than ten miles from shore.

Minutes later Amy hears a frightening sound and feels the blood drain from her face. The plane's rear engine has sputtered for a few seconds, then died. She sees the pilot quickly begin fiddling with his instruments as he swears loudly. Then her stomach turns over as the plane loses altitude.

Looking down at the radio in her lap, she begins an internal debate. Should she contact the Coast Guard? The pilot has not yet radioed their situation, mostly because he's too busy trying to reduce drag, feathering the prop in an attempt to restart the engine and gain altitude. She knows that they still have one good engine, and the pilot has changed course, pointing them west, back toward land. Finally, she thinks, What the hell? And speaks into the radio. "We have lost one engine. Repeat, we have lost one engine."

The Coast Guard answers immediately with questions. How many people onboard? Do you have life jackets? What is your position? With no Loran, Amy is unable to give their exact location. Instead, she tells the Coast Guard approximately how long they have been flying, and their heading. She also remembers seeing what looked to be a large platform buoy. Perhaps a marker indicating the entrance to the Savannah Channel? A few minutes later, as she is listening to the Coast Guard's instructions, she hears a sickeningly familiar sound. The plane's forward engine sputters. Then it dies.

The plane immediately loses altitude, the ocean seemingly rising up to meet it. Masson, finally, gets on his radio to transmit a Mayday call. "Mayday, Mayday, we have lost both engines, repeat we have lost both engines," he says. With no Loran data, he reads his distance mileage equipment and gives more information: "Mayday, Mayday, eighteen east of Savannah, ditching in the water." However, because he had neglected to switch his radio to Channel 16, the marine emergency frequency, the call goes to controllers at Savannah International Airport, not to the Coast Guard.

The plane continues to lose altitude. Fortunately, their Skymaster has retractable landing gear, which will reduce (though not eliminate) the chance that the plane will flip end over end when it hits the water. Masson glides the craft carefully down to the sea, turning into the wind. A veteran of the Canadian Air Force, he's been trained in ditching techniques. He knows that he must try to land on the backs of any waves, or risk having water immediately crash over the plane, possibly flipping it.

Meanwhile, as the plane passes through three hundred, two hundred, one hundred feet on its way to the ocean, Amy makes her last call to the Coast Guard: "Mayday, Mayday! We have lost both engines! Repeat, we have lost both engines! We are going to ditch. Repeat, we are going to ditch!"

Before she hears a response, the pilot tells his passengers to brace themselves for impact. Amy puts her head down on her lap and covers it with her arms. Seconds later she feels the plane thump and skip across the water, bouncing her and the rest of the group in their seats. Dismayed, Amy sees water shooting through the wheel well as if from a fire hose, quickly filling the cabin. After ten seconds the plane stops, and the water is already past their calves. The plane is sinking, she knows, and too quickly. If they don't get out now, they will almost certainly drown.

The pilot reaches across Rachel and tries to open the door. Because of the water pressure outside, it does not budge. As the plane begins to sink, nose up, Amy thinks for the first time about not making it, about drowning, trapped in the tiny cabin. My God, she thinks, the water is cold! Now she sees Brian kicking the door with his bare foot, cutting it badly on the metal. Finally the door moves away from the cabin, sending the ocean rushing into the plane. She is going to have to swim out, underwater, to make it. Panic grips her as she thinks about getting caught, her clothes hung up on something, unable to break free.

She looks toward Brian, in the rear of the plane. He is almost completely submerged now, the water rising to his neck. Thinking that he might not make it, he throws the still-uninflated raft forward, past Amy and toward the cockpit, for someone else to grab. But now it's stuck up front! Rachel, closest to the door, is the first out of the sinking plane. The men yell for Amy to go next. She takes a deep breath, then plunges beneath the surface, swimming through the icy water, through the open doorway of the plane, and then up to the surface. She's made it! Treading in the fifty-degree water, freezing to the bone, she looks back at the plane. The cabin is completely submerged; only the high wings are visible. Then she sees a head pop up to the surface, quickly followed by another. Scott and Brian have made it out.

Seconds pass, with members of the group yelling back and forth across the frigid water. Everyone is okay! But then they quickly realize their mistake. Where is the pilot? And where is the life raft?

◉

Amy's final radio message had been heard by a number of listeners, including the U.S. Coast Guard Station at Hunter Army Airfield and a freighter anchored several miles offshore, near the Savannah Channel beacon. It had also been monitored by Jerry Burleson, a radio operator who was off duty but, by chance, happened to be at the radio at the Charleston Coast Guard Base in South Carolina.

Based on Amy's call, at 12:33 P.M. the Coast Guard dispatched a helicopter to initiate the search for the downed plane. (Marine and Navy aircraft and Coast Guard cutters would follow.) The helicopter, manned by Lieutenant Gary Smith, the pilot; Third Class Aviation Machinist Mate Jeff Ross; and Lieutenant Junior Grade Brad Bean, began to search the waters just off the coast. The ocean was choppy and cold, Smith knew, and with the fifteen-knot wind that had been blowing all morning, the survivors—if there were any—would not last long in the open water.

But there were other problems. The only information at hand was sketchy. Savannah air traffic controllers had radioed the Coast Guard that, according to Masson's initial Mayday call, the plane was "eighteen east of Savannah" and they were "ditching in the water." But the Savannah Airport is more than eighteen miles inland, which would have put the plane over land. What were they "eighteen east" of?

Perhaps Masson had been giving an estimate of their mileage from Tybee Light, a radio beacon at the entrance to the Savannah River. But what was their heading? Without more precise data, the rescue team was unable to narrow their search field. They did not know how far east of the coast the plane had been, or how far west it had gotten before crashing. They also had no idea how far north or south the plane had gone before turning toward shore. Without this information, their task was exponentially more difficult.

And things got worse. The freighter had radioed the Coast Guard, indicating that they had seen the plane heading *west* from the channel beacon, or inland. Though they were unable to pinpoint the precise time of their sighting, it had not been long before Amy's radio call. This information seemed to fit with Masson's initial information that they were "eighteen east of Savannah," which is virtually on the sand. The Coast Guard called the police department at Tybee, a barrier island just off the coast, and asked them to check the beach for signs of the plane. The pilots focused their search on the area near the Tybee beacon and the Georgia coastline.

Jerry Burleson, though he was monitoring the radio more than a hundred miles away in Charleston, intuitively felt the search might be in the wrong place. Burleson had come in to the base on his day off to finish up some paperwork and had heard Amy's distress call over the radio in a nearby room. Although her Mayday call had not given precise coordinates, Burleson felt there was something more to be gained from it. "The information just did not settle well with me," he later recalled. "It was just a feeling that something was wrong."

Sitting at the radio monitoring station, he replayed the tape of her recorded emergency transmission over and over again. There was something there, he felt, something in the background. Fiddling with his controls, he increased the volume until the background noise was audible. A voice! There was someone talking in the background! Listening closely, Burleson determined that he was hearing the pilot speak into the plane's radio just as Amy was making her own transmission. (No one else had heard the voice; Burleson referred to the incident as "just pure luck.") The pilot was reading mileage from his distance-measuring equipment and giving a radius reading from his VORTAC, a much more precise set of data.

Burleson immediately radioed Lieutenant Smith, the helicopter pilot, relaying the information he'd gleaned from the tape. "Do you know where that might be?" Burleson asked. "Will go to that position" was Smith's reply. The Savannah VOR, a navigation station used by pilots, is located in the Savannah Wildlife Refuge, north of the Savannah Airport and a few miles west of the Georgia coast. Masson's VORTAC readings indicated that he was more than twenty-eight nautical miles from the VOR station, which would have put the plane ten miles from the coast, beyond Tybee Island. The Coast Guard quickly altered the search grid, shifting its aircraft and ships to the east, farther out into the Atlantic.

In the ocean, there is still no sign of the pilot, and time is running out. Amy struggles to stay afloat in the freezing water as waves crash over her head. It has been barely two minutes since the plane hit the water, yet she watches despondently as their Skymaster quickly sinks, first the remaining portion of the cabin, then the wings and tail. How could it go so quickly? Suddenly she sees something shoot to the surface from the area of the plane. It's the bright yellow of the life raft. Seconds after it, the head of George Masson pops up. They are all alive.

The men carefully swim away from the sinking plane with the uninflated raft to avoid puncturing it on the wing or one of the propeller blades. When they are at a safe distance, the cord on the raft is pulled and it self-inflates. Fortunately, it seems to be in good shape, and they climb in. Amy, who has been around boats most of her adult life, instantly sees that it is a small, round raft with a rubber bottom, little more than a dinghy—but without an engine. Though it accommodates the group of five, it is not exactly ideal for their conditions. First, it has no cover, nothing to protect them from the chilling effect of the wind. It has no oars. It also has no survival supplies: no food, no blankets, no compass, and no flares, making the chance of a rescue in darkness virtually nonexistent. But the critical thing, and what remains unspoken, is that they have no fresh water. Though they could conceivably last for weeks without food, without water they will die in as little as a few days—assuming hypothermia doesn't kill them first.

It is in the raft, with her first chance to take stock of events, that

Amy begins to panic. What if the Coast Guard did not receive her call? What if no one is looking for them? The air temperature is in the fifties, possibly as high as fifty-five degrees Fahrenheit, and she is freezing, probably mildly hypothermic already. She clutches her wool sweater, now soaked; underneath she has only a short-sleeved shirt. Her feet are ice cold in her wet leather shoes. What will they do when it gets dark, and even colder? Amy starts to lose it, sobbing, the delayed shock of what she has just survived rising to the surface and flooding her with despair. They are going to die out here, on a raft in the ocean, one by one, succumbing to the cold, or to thirst. Or to sharks. No. She puts sharks out of her mind. Though they are certainly a possibility in this area, she knows that they prefer warmer waters. In that sense, at least, the cold water is an advantage.

Scott sees her distress and does his best to comfort her. They are all alive, he says. They made it through a crash at sea! For that alone they should be thankful. And at least Rachel has stopped throwing up! Amy begins to feel better, trying to look on the bright side. Of course someone heard her Mayday call. Or the pilot's. Someone is surely looking for them. Masson, meanwhile, is worried, though not about their condition. He's just lost a plane! And one that wasn't even his! Plus, he knows the plane was not insured. What will he tell Dr. Tedrick?

They begin to discuss the accident, speculating about what might have gone wrong, about their amazing luck that no one has been injured. Well, badly injured anyway. Brian's foot was cut deeply on the plane's door, and the salt water hasn't helped it. But for the most part, they are okay. The pilot tries to perk them up, offering to lead the group in some songs, but no one feels much like singing. After about half an hour, they all look up as one: They hear the roar of a jet passing overhead. But it's just a commercial airliner, miles above, too high to have seen them.

About half an hour later, they look up again. A jet, flying fast and very low, comes over the horizon, then disappears just as quickly. Masson jumps up in the raft and begins shouting and waving but is told to sit down by the others; there's no way the plane could have seen them from that distance. But they are hopeful that it might be a Coast Guard jet on a search pattern. The jet makes three more passes, back and forth, back and forth, until, when it's less than a quarter mile away, they see the pilot tip his wings, indicating he has seen them. Then the plane disappears into the distance. They have been on the raft for two hours.

Minutes later they hear a roar as an orange-striped Coast Guard rescue helicopter approaches the raft from the west. The chopper hovers above the raft for a few seconds, the rotor wash freezing them in their soggy clothing, then moves off to the side. The group sees a stretcher-type basket being lowered on a cable, but it's much too far away for them to reach. What is the pilot doing? Scott, who had worked on a whale-watching boat in Boston, remembers when a sick passenger was airlifted off the ship. The helicopter pilot had first dunked the rescue cage in the water to eliminate any static charge that may have built up in the metal basket. He tells the others that, had the pilot forgotten to dunk the basket, the first person to grab it might have been electrocuted. As it is, when the basket is lowered to the raft he gets a mild shock.

With the basket able to accommodate only one person at a time, Rachel is the first to climb in. She is unceremoniously dunked into the freezing Atlantic, presumably for the reason Scott had described, then hoisted up to the helicopter. Amy is next, followed by the men.

Inside, they are given blankets and asked about their condition. As the chopper heads toward shore, a Coast Guard vessel is sent to retrieve the life raft.

Back at the Coast Guard station, a crowd of reporters has gathered. The group members are offered dry clothing and checked by a doctor, who determines that they are all mildly hypothermic, though not seriously injured. They are allowed time to rewarm and then asked to give a press conference. Masson indicates that he lost power when he attempted to switch from one set of fuel tanks to another, and praises the group for not panicking. After the press conference he gets a pilot friend to fly them all back to Amelia Island. Amy is nervous about getting on the plane, and is an anxious flyer for the rest of the surveying season.

The remainder of the year's survey flights stay within five miles of shore. And Amy begins carrying a waterproof radio on her trips.

◉

What caused both of the plane's engines to fail? Unfortunately, the evidence is inconclusive. Although it went down in just forty feet of water, the Skymaster was deemed unrecoverable by a salvage company. (Masson has since died.) There are some hints, however. The fuel and valve systems for each engine on the Skymaster are completely independent of one another. According to one expert, the chances of a mechanical failure causing both engines to fail almost simultaneously are "astronomically low."

But, as the problem on the previous flight may have indicated, it is entirely possible that the selector valve on the rear engine was faulty. This could have easily caused the engine to fail from fuel starvation: It would have been trying to draw fuel from the empty auxiliary tank. At this point, Amy says Masson tried to feather the prop. Even with one engine still operating, the plane would have been losing altitude, and since it was already low, Masson had very little time to act. Under pressure, he may have accidentally feathered the front engine instead of the rear, which would have caused the plane immediately to lose too much altitude to make an engine restart possible.

Another possible scenario is that the plane was not fully fueled. All pilots of small planes know not to rely on their fuel gauges. But because of the Skymaster's complex fuel system, owner-pilots of the plane "never, ever, ever go on their fuel gauges," one Skymaster pilot with decades of flying experience says. "They measure how much fuel they put in, and calculate their flying time carefully." Masson, who did not own the plane, may have been unaware of its fuel system quirks and thus calculated his flying time incorrectly. Or he may not have fueled the plane himself.

Another possibility is that, after taking off, Masson did not fly on the main tanks long enough to substantially deplete them of fuel, leaving room for the excess routed from the auxiliaries. This would have shortened his flying time on the rear engine considerably. After the rear engine failed, he may have inadvertently switched the plane's front engine to the off position when he thought he was switching it from aux to main. Again, in this plane this mistake is not especially uncommon. Yet another possibility is that he forgot to activate the boost pump when he switched tanks on the rear engine. This pump accelerates fuel delivery from a new tank when a switch is made. If he forgot to activate the pump, he may have panicked when the engine did not restart immediately and, in his confusion, switched back to the empty tank.

Whatever the cause of the crash, Masson was able to ditch the plane correctly, and he brought the life raft. Both actions probably saved his life, and the lives of his passengers.

❖

Would the group have been found had Amy not brought her radio? Would the Coast Guard have discovered the raft had Jerry Burleson decided not to come in to work on his day off? Or had he not experienced "a feeling" that there was more to be gained from Amy's distress call?

The answers are impossible to know, of course. But until Jerry's radio call, the Coast Guard was searching miles from the ditch site. In January, it would have gotten dark at about five o'clock. A few extra hours and the group would have had little hope of rescue before dawn. Those hours could easily have resulted in someone's death by hypothermia.

Clearly, Amy's and Jerry's initial emotional responses to their situations played critical roles in their later decisions, which opened the door for the good luck that followed. But this outcome seems to be consistent with findings that "gut" feelings, experienced at the moment a decision occurs, can play a critical role in the choice one makes. Further, researchers argue, initial or "anticipatory" emotions not only can be used in risky situations but also can be applied to any type of decision.

Is the experience of such emotions equivalent to "intuition"? Should we trust intuition to bring us good luck, or help us avoid bad luck? Research on the phenomenon of intuition is ongoing, although emotion is distinct from cognition, which may play a larger role in intuition. Nevertheless, it does appear that it pays to trust your instincts when it comes to assessing risks, and to use your gut feelings to act accordingly. As Amy found out, trusting her instincts—both to bring the radio and to make those critical calls to the Coast Guard—opened the door for her rescue. Even (perhaps especially) in situations of uncertainty, choices made on the basis of good risk assessment are likely to result in more favorable results.

CHAPTER 6

It Is Not a Log

Josh Smith is freezing, desert sand is stinging his face, and he's try-ing to find some bones.

It's February 1999 in the Western Desert of Egypt, a half day's fast drive out of Cairo, and his Toyota Land Cruiser is crunching over the wind-blasted, hard-packed sand of the parched desert floor. Josh is in the passenger's seat, riding shotgun, his head out the open window, peering at a mind-numbingly endless beige landscape, hop-ing to find something, anything to make this journey worthwhile. Jen, his girlfriend and fellow doctoral candidate, is in the back, moni-toring the Global Positioning System; Dr. Robert Giegengack, her adviser, is driving their rented 4 × 4. Fast.

For Egyptian artifacts, Josh knows, the deserts surrounding Cairo are a gold mine. But for dinosaur hunters like him, the Western Desert is still a relative mystery: Excavation permits are difficult to

come by, cultural differences in the Muslim world can cause misun-
derstandings, and the harsh desert climate means only a few months
of the year are amenable for digging. And the digging is hard. The
winds constantly blow any loose sand particles, leaving a well-
scrubbed landscape of hard-packed earth and rock. As a result, little
is known about the dinosaurs that once roamed this former swamp,
75 million years before it became a desert.

But now they've finally made it, and they've found nothing.

Josh smiles to himself, his mind drifting back to the dusty volume
he had chanced upon a few days before. The book, a British discussion of the paleontology of the Bahariya Oasis (mostly by French and
German paleontologists), had been written in the 1950s. It had described a number of important dinosaur discoveries, including several
significant finds at Gebel el Dist, a natural rock pyramid, the area
around which was excavated in 1911 by the German explorer Ernst
Stromer von Reichenbach. Critically, the book mentioned Stromer's
map coordinates for one locality. Lost for almost a century, the actual
locations of the excavation sites were the stuff of paleontology lore,
and Josh was well aware of their significance. When he saw the coordinates, it was as though he had come across a map to buried treasure.

But if there *is* some fossil treasure out here, Josh and his team
can't locate it. They have found exactly nothing, not even the Gebel
el Dist, much less any bones. Perhaps Stromer got the coordinates
wrong. Or perhaps the desert landscape has changed, obscuring the
quarry area. Frustrated and dejected, Josh peers out of the Land
Cruiser as they circle and crisscross the baked ground. Minute after
minute, the miles tick away. Josh is about to give up hope when, out
of nowhere, something in the sand makes him turn. It's a long, dark
object, ten, perhaps fifteen feet from them, maybe a burned log, pos-

sibly used for fuel by a nomad or other desert traveler. Whatever it is, it looks out of place. "Stop!" he yells, and Giegengack slams on the brakes. The three quickly pile out and walk over, kneeling around the log. Josh and Jen exchange an excited glance, and both quickly realize that what they have found is not a log. It's a bone.

Having rested by itself for millennia, seemingly dropped here on the surface of nowhere, surrounded by aeons of drifting sand, swirling winds, and scorched rock, a blackened dinosaur bone sits. And it is huge.

❋

Throughout history, chance and timing have played important roles in science and discovery, from the extinction of the dinosaurs through the fortuitous winds in Columbus's sails to the random nugget of gold at Sutter's Mill. Being in "the right place at the right time" can be a powerful revelatory force even when, as in Columbus's case, you don't know precisely what it is you've stumbled upon. Indeed, the very unstructured process of exploration almost inevitably leads to unexpected results, some lucky, some unlucky—and some both lucky (for Columbus) and unlucky (for American Indians) at the same time. Some researchers even argue that "unexpected, important events are most likely to be observed when the inquiry is open and flexibly structured."

But how, exactly, does luck operate in the scientific discovery process? Louis Pasteur famously remarked that "in the field of observation, chance favors only the prepared mind." In science, it seems, turning a random event into a piece of good luck requires more than simple discovery. It demands not just favorable external conditions but also an internal process of recognition, organization, and analysis.

It also requires self-confidence, and the courage of one's convictions. And, at least in Josh Smith's case, the paths leading both to and from the lucky event appear to demand a broad range of social and professional connections. As one observer notes, "Much that is considered 'luck' is probably the operation of 'knowing the right people' and being in 'the right' communication channels."

Thus, even in the seemingly organized, predictable world of science—where rigorous standards of evidence are strictly enforced—the search for one piece of information can lead one to discover, by chance, an even more important one. Josh Smith's story of dinosaur discovery illustrates a number of the characteristics of making the most out of a good-luck event. These include being able to recognize immediately particular objects and situations, quickly processing and fitting them into an overall pattern or framework of understanding; possessing a broad knowledge base in one's chosen field of study or occupation; and maintaining a wide social and professional circle of people with varied interests.

❀

It is in the late months of 1914 that Dr. Ernst Stromer von Reichenbach of the University of Munich begins to get worried. Even out here in the parched desert landscape of northwest Egypt, thousands of miles from Europe, he hears the rumblings of war. On July 28, 1914, just a month after the assassination of Archduke Francis Ferdinand in Sarajevo, Austria-Hungary had declared war on Serbia, and World War I had begun. In November, Britain declared war on the Ottoman Empire and in December proclaimed a protectorate over Egypt.

Stromer knows that, because of its strategic location on the northern tip of the African continent, Egypt will be heavily contested in the battles to come. A wealthy baron with a family estate and large castle in Nürnberg, Stromer is short, dark-haired, and full-bearded, with an intense gaze behind small eyeglasses. Wondering what the future holds for him, for his family, and for his important work, the geologist looks wistfully up at Gebel el Dist, the peculiarly majestic rock formation at the base of which he and his team have made so many important discoveries.

Three years before, Stromer and his Egyptian assistants had set out on camelback from Cairo, riding nearly two hundred miles south-southwest across this windblown desert to the outpost known as the Bahariya Oasis, a trickle of life in an otherwise barren expanse. The towering rock formation at the base of which he now sits—composed of the rocks of the Bahariya Formation—has been a treasure trove of discoveries for the young geologist-paleontologist. Quarries that he and his team have dug into the soft sand and hard rock surrounding the formation have produced dozens of finds dating back to the Cretaceous period, nearly 100 million years ago. These discoveries, he is certain, will alter the known landscape of African paleontology for years, perhaps decades, to come.

Stromer's expeditions have recovered a diverse range of fossils—ocean reptiles, invertebrates, plants, and huge plant eaters, including an enormous sauropod that probably weighed fifty tons and was twenty to thirty yards long. He imagines what this area was like, so long ago, when beasts of such might roamed the earth, tens of millions of years before humankind appeared. How majestic these creatures must have looked! Stepping with feet nearly two yards in length, they would have moved slowly, searching for plants to eat in these swamps, since the fossil record shows that the area was a humid coastal plain at that time. What caused these animals, the biggest ever to have roamed the earth, to disappear so long ago?

But now his thoughts turn to the present as he wraps his dusty fossils in plaster-soaked burlap for their long journey back to Munich. With trepidation, Stromer looks to the sky and thinks of war. Perhaps he imagines one of the new air machines he's heard about, flying over Gebel el Dist itself and dropping its payload of TNT on the site, burying in the sand once again the discoveries he has worked for three years to uncover.

In an instant, he becomes deathly afraid that his important work will be lost, making further critical study impossible. A fit of panic grips him, and he reaches for his diary, jotting down the exact latitude and longitude of his excavation pits. He's recorded the coordinates before, of course. But as a researcher, Stromer knows all too well the value of being meticulous: If his maps should somehow be lost, or his research destroyed, well, he knows the more information that exists about the site, the better the chances of future explorers coming back.

He wipes the dirt and grit from his glasses just as a cold wind drifts into the camp, stinging his face with fine sand grains. Stromer peers through his streaked spectacles toward the horizon, checking fearfully for an approaching sandstorm. But all he sees is the shimmering sand. Feeling a chill on his neck, he suddenly realizes the weather is changing. Soon the freezing winds of winter will be upon them.

Some thirty years later, thousands of miles away, at the end of a different war and in a bitter piece of bad luck, Stromer's worst fears will be realized. His decades of labor and research—a lifetime, really—will disappear for nearly half a century: his excavations lost, his fossils pounded to dust, his historic research destroyed. His work and his name will undergo a slow transformation, from reality to rumor and, ultimately, to legend, a legacy that might have remained buried under the sand and in the history books if not for a stroke of incredible luck.

◉

Josh Smith is drinking beer at Philadelphia's New Deck Tavern and listening to Matt Lamanna explain his spreadsheet. It is the fall of 1997, and Josh has just completed his master's in geology at the University of Pennsylvania. Matt, an eager, somewhat intense new grad student in Josh's department, is in the middle of describing what, in Josh's view, is a fairly anal (but nonetheless useful) piece of research.

Though Josh isn't aware of it, Matt knows, the two men's paths have crossed before—just one more in a long line of amazing coincidences that make up their shared story. As an undergraduate in 1995, Matt had been on a dig at the Lance Formation, the site in Wyoming where the first *Tyrannosaurus rex* fossils had been found. Stumbling upon a new bone accumulation, Matt thought he might have made an important discovery at the site, possibly even three new *T. rex* fossils. Unfortunately, his season was coming to an end, and he did not have time for the full excavation.

Later that year he contacted Kraig Derstler, of the University of New Orleans, under whom he had been working. "Did anything ever happen with that Lance Formation site I found?" he asked.

"Actually, yes. A brash young guy from the University of Pennsylvania came after you and started poking around. He never found anything." What was the guy's name, Matt wanted to know.

"Josh Smith" was Derstler's reply.

Now the two are in the same department at Penn, working together to find promising new research sites. It isn't easy. Matt has become frustrated with all the sites currently being excavated. Perusing a 1990 list of all known dinosaur finds, he has discovered that most have already been picked clean, and therefore finding anything new will be next to impossible. Josh knows that Matt is simply looking for something interesting and new to research, but he's obviously put a lot of time into this thing, so Josh orders them another round and listens.

"Bahariya Oasis," Matt pronounces. "That's the place."

"Bahariya?" Josh says incredulously. "Stromer's site? In Egypt? How's that going to happen?"

Using the 1990 report as a guide, Matt had created his own list, a spreadsheet of fifty of the world's dinosaur digs that had produced hints of exciting new finds, but were not currently being excavated. Using a five-point scale he's devised, Matt had ranked each site based on its desirability as a dig location, including its potential as a source of new fossils. Bahariya had come up as one of the more promising. Because of Stromer's finds, they know that dinosaurs once roamed the area. But since the site has not been excavated for decades, there might be significant fossils still in the ground.

At six feet tall and a solid 175 pounds, the blond-haired, blue-eyed Josh relishes the thought of getting out in the desert. As a member of the National Guard infantry for six years, a commitment that paid for his schooling, he learned some field skills that have served him well on a number of paleontological digs. Though just twenty-eight, Josh has plenty of experience doing fieldwork, or at least enough to know the cost, permitting process, and logistical hurdles involved in sending an American team to dig in the Egyptian desert. This is part of the reason that Egypt is still a relatively open book where dinosaur fossils are concerned. With so many good sites in North America, paleontologists think, why bother going halfway around the world?

Still, he's intrigued. Every young dinosaur student knows Stromer's story, almost a fable, really: his amazing finds early in the century, including *Aegyptosaurus,* a titanosaurid, the long-necked, plant-eating dinosaur species (which includes the well-known *Brontosaurus* or *Apatosaurus*), as well as three *Tyrannosaurus*-size theropods, *Spinosaurus, Carcharodontosaurus,* and *Bahariasaurus. Spinosaurus aegyptiacus* was a fearsome-looking animal with a snout like a crocodile's and dorsal spines as much as six feet high.

But Josh also knows the disappointing ending to Stromer's legendary story, how all his records, including the location of the excavation site within the Bahariya Oasis, had been lost or burned. And anyway, going to North Africa is a major expedition, especially for two grad students, neither of whom has yet earned a doctorate. "We'll never get the money," he notes dourly. "And anyway, how would we find it?"

Matt knows Josh is right, of course, and the two halfheartedly discuss a few of the other sites on his spreadsheet, only to end the evening with a good buzz but no clear plan of action for finding a suitable dig site.

The fall and winter of 1997 pass with no progress on getting to Bahariya, and while not forgotten, the trip is on the back burner, with both men involved in their various research interests. Then, in the spring of 1998, a striking piece of luck falls in their laps. A new doctoral candidate at Penn has begun research in the Egyptian desert, looking for evidence of climate change and hominid habitation. She had been to the area earlier that year, but now she needs to return, and her research adviser can't accompany her. Because Egypt is a Muslim country, cultural differences can make it difficult for a female researcher to study there without an accompanying male relative. Thus, she needs a male research partner, the best-case scenario being a husband or a brother, to make the trip with her. The young woman also happens to be dating Josh Smith, whom she met as an undergrad at Harvard. Her name? Jennifer Smith. They can travel as husband and wife, and no one will be the wiser.

The striking coincidence is just too great to pass up. After some haggling with his dissertation adviser, Peter Dodson, Josh gets permission to go with Jen for a five-week research trip in January 1999. There is just one logistical problem. Her research area is in the Dakhla Oasis, in southern Egypt, while the Bahariya Oasis is to the west. Quickly, Josh secures a map of the area, trying to determine if there is some route to his destination that isn't too far out of the way—after all, this is Jen's research trip, not his. As luck would have it, the only road from Cairo to the Dakhla Oasis passes right through Bahariya. Ecstatic, the two plan to spend two to three days working at Gebel el Dist and Stromer's quarries.

Now all they have to do is find them.

❋

It is January 1999, and Josh Smith and Jen Smith, along with Jen's adviser, Bob Giegengack, are eating very sweet, nutty pastries and drinking hot tea with Bahay Issawi in his Cairo home. The team has been in Egypt for a week, gathering permits, securing gear, and just generally getting acclimated. They've even taken some time to see the pyramids and other tourist attractions before setting off for the desert. Issawi is the former head of the Egyptian Geological Survey and Mining Authority, the country's equivalent to the U.S. Geological Survey. The four are discussing the coming weeks of work when Josh mentions they will be stopping at the Bahariya Oasis on their way south. It is then that Giegengack recalls that Issawi had done his master's research on mapping the area and wonders if their host has any maps or information that may be of use. While none of his maps pinpoints Stromer's finds, Issawi remembers something, excuses himself, and returns a few minutes later with an old, dusty book. He hands it to Josh, who begins to read.

The book, written in the mid-1950s, is a British history of the British, French, and German paleontologists who had excavated in Egypt from the late 1800s to about 1935. When Josh turns to the section on Ernst Stromer, his eyes begin to wander, finally settling at the bottom of a page. His heart skips a beat as he sees, plain as day, Stromer's coordinates for the location of his major dinosaur finds. He's found the spot! Grabbing a pen, Josh scribbles the numbers on a slip of paper. With their Global Positioning System, the team should have no problem pinpointing Gebel el Dist. And anyway, the rock is hundreds of feet high, making it easy to spot in the Bahariya Oasis, the lowest section of land in the country.

It's a few days later when the team piles all their gear into the Land Cruiser and drives into the empty expanse of the Bahariya. The weather is cool, even cold, with average temperatures in the forties and a strong wind making it feel even colder outside the confines of the truck. With Bob driving and Jen in the back monitoring the GPS, Josh constantly scans the horizon, looking for Gebel el Dist. Stromer had described an isolated, pyramid-shaped mountain in the desert, but as the three approach his coordinates, nothing matching the description is visible anywhere.

Finally, Josh thinks he sees something, perhaps a low mountain range, to the southeast. But as they drive closer, he sees that it is only a ridge of rock poking out of the sand, perhaps two miles long and five hundred feet high. Frustrated, he begins scanning the sand. He just doesn't understand it. Where are the quarries? Where are the telltale signs of excavation? Giegengack says that something of Stromer's sites should be visible, even after decades of shifting sand. He mentions having seen crusted tank tracks, presumably from Rommel's march across the desert during the Axis's North African campaign during World War II. Certainly if tracks are visible, Josh thinks, huge excavation pits should be easy to spot. But still, nothing.

Driving around aimlessly in the desert, Josh smiles grimly as he recalls Stromer's terrible luck. Forced to shut down his excavation operations by the advance of the First World War, the paleontologist shipped his spectacular fossils to Munich. Then, with deep regret, he abandoned his site to history.

For the next twenty-four years, he worked with his finds. He carefully measured, photographed, and preserved the dinosaur fossils until 1938, when politics made his work at the museum in Munich impossible. An outspoken critic of the rising Nazi regime, Stromer was forced into early retirement, retreating to Grünsburg, his family's castle in Nürnberg, and leaving his life's work at the Alte Akademie, the home of the Bavarian State Collection for Paleontology and Historical

Geology. Then, in April 1944, the Alte Akademie and all Stromer's discoveries were reduced to rubble by an RAF bombing raid. Though the damage was collateral, the building and its contents were gone. None of Stromer's maps or photographs had been recovered, Josh knew, and as a result the excavation site was reclaimed by the desert.

But will finding his site prove impossible? Josh is beginning to think so. The Western Desert comprises two-thirds of the land surface of Egypt, covering about 263,000 square miles. While the area gets minimal rainfall, the landscape changes in other ways. In summer, cyclones blow in *khamsins,* or dust storms, which are caused by southern tropical air moving northward from Sudan. Such storms can bury fossils and landmarks alike, Josh knows, making the discovery of a small piece of bone in the desert a challenge, to say the least.

As they continue driving in circles, Jen spots an outcropping of hills to the northwest. Bob points the truck in their direction and floors it, sending a spray of dust and dirt behind them as they shoot across the desert floor. Staring out the window, Josh suddenly sees the burnt log and yells for them to stop. His initial reaction that what he is seeing is wood, not bone, is not without merit. Because of the ground's high iron content, fossils on the surface become oxidized, giving them the appearance of petrified wood. But as soon as he reaches the object, Josh knows he's found a fossil.

As they gather around, the three scientists immediately see that the bone is broken into three fragments, with the largest section about two feet long and eight inches in diameter. It is quite obviously not hollow, Josh observes, and this realization tempers his excitement somewhat; he's probably found a sauropod. In the highly competitive world of paleontology, the discovery of a meat eater engenders much more excitement in the field. It also gets much more play in the press and, Josh knows, almost always attracts more grant money. Instead, he's found a plant eater. While unearthing one of Stromer's plant-eating sauropods would still be quite a coup, it's not precisely what he has been hoping for. Anyway, this site is obviously not one of Stromer's excavation pits. In fact, the three note, there's no evidence of human presence whatsoever. Just a bunch of blackened dinosaur bones in the middle of the middle of nowhere.

Excited, yet weary and beginning to lose concentration, Josh and his crew dutifully map the bone accumulations using their GPS, take photos and make some diagrams, then resume their drive toward Jen's rock formation. As they get close, they begin to see the tantalizing outline of a tall, cone-shaped peak. But they also realize that daylight is running out. They decide to renew their search for Gebel el Dist the following day, February 22. But time, Josh knows, is running out. If they don't find Stromer's quarries soon, they will have to continue south to the Dakhla Oasis to begin Jen's sedimentation studies.

❁

The next day, Josh, Jen, and Bob leave their Bawiti hotel early in the morning, once again piling themselves and all their gear into the dust-covered Land Cruiser. This time, they take no chances. Heading out to the rock formation they had spotted the day before, they stop to talk to a man watering his camel. Is that Gebel el Dist, they want to know, gesturing to the pointed rock tower in the distance. The man confirms that it is the right formation. They have found Stromer's site.

The team spends the entire day excavating a huge number of bone accumulations. "There were just piles of bones everywhere," Josh recalls. He finds a number of large, hollow bones—predators!—

as well as piles of semiburied sauropod fossils, fish, and even a croco-dilelike species. "It was a very big deal," he says. After two days of mapping and photographing their excavations, the team, exhilarated, heads south. But neither Josh Smith nor his team knows that the biggest find, the one that will put them on national television and in newspapers around the world, and will get them highly coveted by-lines in the magazine *Science,* has yet to be unearthed. It is still sitting on the surface of the desert, looking for all the world like a petrified log, right where Josh had seen it three days before.

◉

Matt is in his office on the third floor of Hayden Hall, on the Penn campus, when he hears a familiar *clomp clomp* up the stairs. It is Febru-ary 1999. He turns, and as expected, Josh is standing in the doorway, grinning ear to ear. He's also disgusting: sweaty, dusty, smelly, and with a scraggly "field beard" from his weeks in the desert. He obviously has come here, to their office, before even going home to shower.

"What?" Matt says, his green eyes glowing. "You found some-thing! What did you find?"

Josh shows him photos of a hollow bone, as well as pictures of very large bone fragments that could only have come from an enor-mous sauropod. Matt's spreadsheet had been right: Bahariya was in-deed a gold mine for the two young paleontologists.

But how to get back? Josh and Matt try desperately to find a way to mount a return expedition. Again, the problem is money. The two figure it will take a team of excavators at least several weeks—and tens of thousands of dollars—to fully uncover, map, photograph, and remove the huge number of fossils remaining at Gebel el Dist. Josh spends the next few months attempting to get the necessary financing, but he comes up with nothing.

Then, one night later that summer, comes another lucky break. Josh is having a few beers with Scott Winters, a fellow Ph.D. candidate at Penn, telling him the story of his, and Stromer's, discoveries. Winters is intrigued. He's also well connected, serving as a partner in a Los Angeles–based film production company called Last Word Productions that specializes in science documentaries. Hearing the details of Josh's discovery story, he immediately understands its cinematic possibilities: a return expedition to the remote Western Desert, the parallel stories of Smith and Stromer—two researchers, one lucky, one unlucky—on the trail of the largest creatures that ever walked the earth. Would Josh be willing, Winters wants to know, to grant the rights to film the expedition in return for funding it? For, say, fifty thousand dollars? Josh agrees immediately. Eventually, Winters brokers a deal to bring in MPH Entertainment, a larger company with more financial resources.

The next six months are spent securing the necessary entry and excavation permits, getting all the logistics in place, and gathering and training the personnel who will be making the trip. Finally, in January 2000, Josh, Matt, a team of researchers, and the film crew—twenty-one people in all—leave for Cairo and then Bawiti, deep in the Bahariya Oasis. With Josh's photos and the GPS coordinates of Stromer's quarries, they intend to continue where Stromer left off almost a century before, locating and unearthing fossilized remains that have been buried for nearly a million centuries.

The trip, however, starts badly. The weather is not cooperating: Daytime temperatures are hovering around the freezing mark, making digging into the stone floor of Bahariya even more difficult. The group is beset by numerous sandstorms, and soon many members of the team come down with food poisoning. ("It was awful," Josh remembers. "Plus we just weren't finding anything that interesting.") While the group has clearly found Stromer's original quarries, they are continually digging up fragmented clues, not intact specimens. Many of the bones uncovered are not pieces of complete fossilized remains but rather partial remains, skeletons that had been blown to pieces over aeons by the harsh desert winds. ("The first weeks were really, really bad," Josh recalls. "We found some cool things, but nothing that would 'pay the bills.' ")

There were other pressures as well. With the film crew recording their every move, the team felt even more urgency to find something, anything, that would make the long, expensive journey worthwhile. Matt remembers that at one point the crew began to shut off their cameras to save film. When the young paleontologists would dig up a bone, the filmmakers would make them reenact the discovery for the tape, even adding hokey dialogue to enhance the "authenticity" of the filmed segment.

They have been digging for three weeks.

Finally, on January 27, in near-desperation, Josh Smith takes a gamble. Rather than continue to struggle at Stromer's site, he decides to return to the site of that blackened dinosaur bone viewed by chance from the Land Cruiser. Using his GPS data, Josh, Matt, and their fellow team member Jason Poole drive across the floor of the Bahariya Oasis to the spot where the first bone had been spotted. Radio in hand, Matt wanders off to another promising bone accumulation, while Josh and Jason begin to dig. After several hours, Matt hears the radio crackle with Josh's voice. "Matt," says the disembodied voice, "you gotta come over here. Now."

The year before, Josh had been certain that the animal he found had been one of the sauropod species Stromer had discovered. But when Matt approaches Josh and Jason, he sees that whatever they have found is too big to be one of Stromer's animals. The bone, nearly six feet in length, could be only one thing: "It's a humerus," Josh says, or upper arm bone. (The bone functioned as a front leg on the dinosaur.)

But, Matt wonders, how can that be? An animal with a humerus of this size would have been among the largest creatures ever uncovered; Stromer had identified no such dinosaur. This bone looks like it weighs hundreds of pounds. But even more important, Matt sees, it is fossilized with nearly a quarter of the creature's full skeleton, making identification a real possibility. The unspoken question hangs in the air: If this isn't Stromer's sauropod, what is it?

The bones are unearthed and transported to the United States for cleaning and further study. After running the numbers, the team is amazed to find that the animal they have uncovered is a new genus of titanosaurid, a group of long-necked, long-tailed plant eaters that were among the largest animals to have roamed the earth. In fact, the new dinosaur is very close in size to *Argentinosaurus,* the most massive dinosaur ever discovered. Josh and his team decide to name their creature *Paralititan stromeri,* in honor of Ernst Stromer. The name means "tidal giant," since the dinosaur lived—and died—in an area that was a coastal plain. The skeleton they had found was the second or third most complete specimen ever uncovered on the African continent.

○

Its massive size notwithstanding, in general scientific terms, how important was Josh Smith's chance discovery? First, the discovery of any new dinosaur is a major event in paleontology. But more to the point, the time in which *Paralititan* roamed the earth, about 95 million years ago, is considered a critical period in the planet's geological and biological history. The so-called early late-Cretaceous period was "basically the final act of the dinosaurs," Josh notes, adding that knowledge of what North Africa was like at that time is severely limited. "Because of the fossilized remains that he discovered, Stromer knew that it was not desert at the time, that it was a wet, coastal area," he says. "And other research by team geologist Ken Lacovara has indicated that it might have been a mangrove swamp." The research performed by Josh and his team reinforced the view that *Paralititan* had lived and died in an area of mangrove swamp much like what is found today in southern Florida.

And the discovery site and surrounding areas of the desert, unexplored for most of the century before Josh and his team arrived, is still yielding tantalizing clues. These include the possible remains of a "super reptile" that would have dwarfed today's crocodiles and another tantalizing find the paleontologists refuse to discuss.

Both Josh and Matt are quick to credit the almost unbelievable string of luck with playing a critical role in their finds: Two scientists named Smith, a dusty book with some map coordinates, a glance out a speeding truck's window, and a college friend with connections in Hollywood. But, though both young paleontologists are far too modest to say so, it was their ingenuity, their determination, and ultimately their open minds that led to a flexibly structured discovery process, one that vastly increased their chances of success. "The mind must be prepared to receive the germ of a new idea," one researcher has written. "What is 'chance' for the unprepared mind may be a fascinating springboard to new ideas for the prepared mind."

"It seems to me now that as you get your research going," the well-known science author Lewis Thomas once said, "things are bound to begin happening if you've got your wits about you. You create the lucky accidents."

CHAPTER 7

Like a Shotgun Blast Inside the Plane

Keith Gallagher feels death approaching.

His helmet and oxygen mask have just been blown off his head, and now he's trying desperately to duck; he's trying to get out of the way, trying to get out of the wind that is sucking the oxygen from his lungs. With the plane moving at 275 knots, and at 8,000 feet above the sea, he knows that he has just a few seconds before he loses consciousness. In the foggy haze that comes just before blacking out, he turns to look at the pilot of his A-6, who is sitting right beside him. But for some reason, instead of seeing the pilot's knee and hand, as he should be, he's looking at the top of his head. He thinks this is very strange.

He reaches down to pull the ejection handle between his legs. It does not move. He almost laughs at the absurdity of it: half in, half out of a speeding jet, unable to get back in, unable to eject and get out.

He should be panicking, but instead he's wondering at the very odd predicament he finds himself in. And then the blackness begins to creep into his head. He tries to will it away, to keep himself conscious so he can help the pilot land the plane. But it's no use.

He wonders if he will be dead before the plane slams into the Indian Ocean. Or perhaps he will be killed a different way, flying out of the now open cockpit as the pilot lands the plane safely. As he embraces unconsciousness, he thinks that most likely they will both simply slam into the only thing that can possibly save their lives, the deck of the USS *Abraham Lincoln*, the aircraft carrier plowing slowly through the water more than a mile below.

Then the darkness comes, and none of it matters anymore.

◉

The mathematician and author John Allen Paulos relates the tale, probably a fable, of the frequent flyer who is deathly afraid of the remote possibility of a bomb on his plane. Knowing the chances are low—but not low enough for comfort—the man decides he will always travel with a bomb in his suitcase, reasoning that the odds against having two bombs on an airplane would be astronomical.

This story illustrates a widely held belief that even random events must stick to some pattern and thus if we can just know the odds we can in some sense take control of such events, just as the fearful traveler seeks to increase the odds against the unknown cause (a planted bomb exploding) by taking direct action he believes will sway things in his favor (planting his own bomb). The reality, of course, is that the traveler's independent action does not in any way decrease his chances of being on that ill-fated flight (and in fact might increase his chances, if his bomb goes off!). While we may be able to predict some chance events, either through careful study or by chance itself, we cannot do so with any reasonable certainty, which allows for the occurrence of luck.

But is this the only way prediction, preparation, and luck interact? We often believe that the three concepts are at odds: How can one predict chance events? Similarly, how can one prepare for randomness, for the turn of events that could not have been foreseen? And even assuming we knew the odds against (or for) a particular event happening to *someone* at *some time,* how would such knowledge help us to plan for such events happening to us?

By definition, randomness is unknowable in advance, or else its causes are hidden from us to such an extent that preparation for a specific random event is impossible. Thus it would seem that preparation for luck, too, is impossible. How can one prepare for the unpredictable? In fact, on several levels, training and preparation seem to be tied to the ways in which we react to luck, both good and bad. A very specific preparation strategy called "defensive pessimism" may in many cases make us better able to manage the fallout from bad-luck events, and at the same time open the door for good luck. Keith Gallagher's story illustrates the close relationship between luck and preparation, which can mean the difference between life and death.

○

It's July 9, 1991, and the Gulf War has just ended with an unprecedented military victory for the United States and its Operation

Desert Storm coalition. Iraq's army has been routed, even humili-
ated, and now the job of patrolling the Persian Gulf is a bit less
dangerous—and, truth be told, a bit less exciting too. Still, Navy
Lieutenant Keith Gallagher is in a celebratory mood: Today is his
twenty-sixth birthday, and with the crew of the USS *Abraham Lincoln* and its battle group, he's two days out of Singapore, on his way
around the tip of the Indian subcontinent, aiming to rendezvous
with other warships currently in the Gulf region. His carrier group
has missed all of the Gulf War action, but just getting out into open
water, with the potential of some postwar excitement, has Keith and
the rest of the crew members on their toes.

The Navy offers little time for birthday celebrations, of course,
though Keith is expecting a cake when he returns to the ship later in
the day. Right now, he's concentrating on the mission ahead. As a
bombardier-navigator, he will be sitting next to Lieutenant Mark
Baden, the pilot in their Green Lizard KA-6D (an A-6), as the two
men serve as overhead tanker for the *Lincoln.*

"You know," Keith says to Mark, "this will be my hundredth
'trap' on the boat." Both men comment on the fact that, with the one
hundredth trap, Keith's birthday, and the fact that Mark's name happens to be painted on the side of the plane, this is sure to be a good
flight. (Each pilot has his name on one of the carrier's aircraft, and
that day Mark coincidentally happens to be flying the plane with his
name emblazoned on its side.)

But although he doesn't mention it to his navigator, Mark is un-
easy. The ship has had a number of troubling incidents, and it's been
out of port for only a few weeks. Just one day before, off the coast of
Sri Lanka, one of the carrier aircraft had gone into the sea, although

the crew had ejected safely. A few days before that, on July 4, someone had pulled the emergency jettison handle on a parked aircraft, firing the canopy off the plane, onto the deck, and into the sea. Luckily no one had been hurt in that incident, either. And just a few days before that, two craft had been involved in a midair collision, with one crew ejecting safely into the sea and another losing almost ten feet of the starboard wing of their airplane before making an emergency landing in Singapore. While mishaps are not uncommon on a carrier with hundreds of planes and thousands of personnel, so many so close together had the entire crew on edge.

Perhaps for this reason, Mark takes extra precautions before leaving the carrier deck. As the plane taxis out of the chocks and onto the catapult, he begins to go through the "soft shot" EPs, or the emergency procedures should the engine fail on takeoff. As he mentally ticks off one step after another, he casually touches each switch and lever, making sure all are in the proper positions for takeoff. If something happens, he thinks, at least I'll be ready. Then he fires the engines, gives the A-6 full throttle, and the ship's massive catapult launches Keith and Mark off the deck and into the clear blue sky above the Indian Ocean.

❂

Keith, too, knew about the accidents. Though it appeared that none of the mishaps would have been easily preventable by the actions of a naval flight officer, the knowledge of them kept him more focused. "If an accident could have been prevented by checking something on preflight, you better believe I checked it very carefully," he recalls. "Other accidents were a reminder of the dangers involved," he adds, "and they helped to remove complacency. I think that's just human nature."

It's also one important facet of human psychology, and it is becoming well known to researchers. A new field of psychological study is now focusing on an adaptive strategy that may help to explain how some people react to bad luck. This strategy, called "defensive pessimism," is a thought process that helps to turn negative thinking (anxiety) into action. "Anxiety is disruptive," the Wesleyan psychology professor and author Julie Norem says. "It can interfere with performance, and it will interfere more the harder the task is." By using defensive pessimism as a mental preparation strategy, it is possible to overcome the negative effects of bad luck, even in life-threatening situations.

Defensive pessimists, it should be noted, are not especially negative people, nor are they pessimistic about all aspects of their lives. Rather, they use pessimism in a very specific way—and in very specific circumstances—to help them overcome particular types of obstacles. Keith and—especially—Mark used several aspects of defensive pessimism before their fateful flight, including mental rehearsal, a "worst-case scenario" analysis, and the preparation of plans of action should things go wrong. Thus, while predicting bad luck is, of course, impossible, planning for it is not—and, in fact, is prudent. By using defensive pessimism as a planning strategy, we can give ourselves some insurance against bad luck.

◉

Overhead tanker duty (or "tanker hop") is a representative sample of life in the military: brief periods of intense concentration and activity followed by long stretches of mind-numbing boredom. The assignment basically requires the A-6 aircraft to act as a flying fuel pump. Because takeoff and landing cycles on an aircraft carrier burn thousands of pounds of fuel, their plane will connect to and fill up the tanks of planes just before they approach for landing and just after they leave the flight deck. Midair refueling, while relatively commonplace for Navy jets, is nonetheless technically fairly rigorous, and Keith knows that for the first fifteen to twenty minutes of their ninety-minute shift they will be busy. After the wave of planes leave the ship, they will circle repeatedly at eight thousand feet for nearly an hour; then things will perk up again as they refuel the returning planes from the thousands of gallons that sit in their own aircraft's five huge fuel tanks.

The first half of the mission goes without a hitch. While the winds are gusting to almost thirty knots down on the flight deck, the skies are clear and relatively calm this high up. At midcycle, or about forty-five minutes into their flight, they are settled well into the boring stage, making big, lazy circles over the ship and listening to chatter on the radio. At some point both Keith and Mark notice a problem, and they begin a brief discussion.

MARK: You watching that drop tank?
KEITH: Yeah. No fuel transfer?
MARK: Probably the float valve. Let me try to overpressurize.

Both aviators have observed that the fuel in one of the aircraft's right drop tanks is not being transferred to the plane. Though they are concerned, neither man panics. While not completely normal, on this twenty-year-old plane the problem is not exactly unheard of, either; it's generally the result of a stuck float valve. Mark tries switching to override on tank pressurization, hoping this will force the valve to open. It doesn't work.

Finally, both men realize that the problem can be rectified only by "porpoising" the plane. Keith gives Mark a hand motion, indicating that he should begin the porpoise.

The maneuver, which entails increasing airspeed and then quickly changing altitude, is somewhat akin to the motion of a roller coaster—or the movement made by a dolphin as it leaps up and out of the water and then dives back down. Pilots will sometimes "porpoise" simply because it feels cool, just like the G-forces generated on the roller coaster. This time, though, the porpoise will be used to generate positive and negative G-forces and, they hope, create enough pressure to jar the valve loose and back to its proper position. It's a relatively crude but very effective fix for the problem, and pilots of the aircraft know it well.

Mark flicks off the altitude hold, allowing him to change the plane's altitude and airspeed manually, using the yoke. Then he begins the porpoise. When their airspeed reaches 230 knots, Mark pulls back on the stick, moving the plane five degrees nose up. They shoot up into the sky. Quickly, he pushes the stick forward, creating about half of a negative G, or just enough to float the two men in their seats: They feel their stomachs turn over. Suddenly both are aware of a loud bang, almost like a shotgun blast inside the plane, followed immediately by the depressurization of the cockpit and a blast of freezing air. Something has gone terribly wrong.

Keith instantly thinks that the Plexiglas canopy above him has blown off, probably through some malfunction. Now the wind, coming at him while the plane is traveling almost three hundred miles an hour, is making it impossible for him to do anything. Instinctively, he leans forward, trying to get his head below the level of the windscreen, a position he hopes will offer his head and face some limited protection. But it's just no use: The air pressure is blowing him back in his seat as if he's held in place by steel clamps. He can barely move an inch, much less get his head down and out of the path of the wind.

Instinctively, he looks over at Mark. Since he and the pilot sit next to each other, and at the same height, looking down and left should allow him to see the pilot's right knee and hand. What he sees instead—or rather what he does not see—chills him to the bone. He is now looking at the back of Mark's head. Looking farther left, he needs a second to make sense of what he is seeing. Then he realizes that he is peering down at the cockpit from above. Not understanding how such a thing is possible, he finally feels that he is still sitting upright in his seat. He instantly comes to the frightening realization he has somehow partially ejected from the plane. His seat is about three feet above the fuselage, still somehow connected, and the wind is trying to fling him out of the plane.

Mark, meanwhile, looks right, expecting to meet the wondering gaze of his BN. Instead, he sees only Keith's legs, and one side of the plane's canopy. It is shattered. What the hell's happening? Mark thinks, quickly hoping that Keith is able to eject from the plane. An instant later, he realizes that he needs to slow down. He jerks the throttles to idle and starts the speed brakes, hoping to slow the plane quickly. Desperately, he looks at the airspeed indicator: two hundred knots. Still too fast. Mark reaches up and deisolates, activating the hydraulics to the flaps and landing gear, then throws the flap lever to the down position. Then he grabs the IFF selector switch and changes it to EMER, providing the air traffic controllers on the ship with a clear indication of his location and emergency status. Again he checks the airspeed indicator and gives another pull on the throttles and speed brakes. Finally the indicator begin to cross two hundred knots and fall.

Several desperate minutes pass as Keith struggles to find a solution to the wind. Then things get worse. His helmet and oxygen mask are ripped off his face and sent hurtling into the sea, thousands of feet below. Without oxygen, Keith knows that he has a minute or two at most before unconsciousness. The wind is making it impossible to keep his eyes open, and he feels as though someone is holding a fire hose on him from inches away. He realizes his only hope is to fully eject and wait for rescue at sea, assuming he will be able to separate from his seat, so that it does not drag him to the bottom.

With superhuman effort, he reaches down for his ejector handle, fighting against the power of the wind. He pulls up. It does not budge. The partial ejection must have somehow disabled the pancake charge that fires the seat out of the cockpit. Thinking fast, he remembers that there is a second ejection handle by his head, but he cannot move his arm to reach it: the wind is just too strong. Now the air is being sucked from his lungs as if by some giant vacuum. Each breath is a strain, and he starts to panic. He begins to kick on the dashboard, desperately trying to signal for help. As the seconds tick away, the blackness closes in. The kicking slows, then stops completely. Mark knows Keith is dying.

❀

Landing an airplane on an aircraft carrier is one of the most difficult feats in aviation, and even experienced pilots can be (and sometimes are) killed by a small mistake. In ideal conditions, carrier pilots take off and land into the wind. Crosswinds—those blowing across the runway—make a plane more difficult to control. Depending on the direction of the ship and the direction of the wind, the carrier often needs to change course before its planes can land. But moving an enormous ship like an aircraft carrier is no simple task; the process can take many minutes.

And there are further complications. Because carrier-based aircraft do not have enough runway room to slow down and stop using only flaps and reverse engine power, a "hook and wire" system is used. A carrier has four landing wires, which are caught by a tailhook that is trailed by the airplane; the process is called a "trap." The wires are numbered 1 through 4, with wire 1 closest to the rear edge of the deck (planes approach the ship from the back) and the one that the pilot will encounter first upon approach. Wires 2, 3, and 4 are farther down the landing area, giving the pilot three additional chances to engage his tailhook.

While it may seem logical that pilots would attempt to engage the first wire, the goal is generally to catch wire number 3. The logic is that if a pilot tries for wire 1 and comes up short, he has a decent chance of slamming into the "round down," or the rear edge of the flight deck at the stern of the ship. Wire 4, of course, is the last-chance wire, and if the tailhook does not engage the other wires and then misses number 4, the pilot will have to make another landing attempt. Wires 2 and 3 get the plane away from the leading edge of the runway yet still leave at least one backup wire to catch the tailhook if there's a miss. (Since the hook may miss a wire, hit the deck, and then bounce up, having a backup wire is a necessity.)

There are other difficulties, too. Unlike other pilots, carrier pilots apply full throttle to their engines the instant their wheels touch the surface of the runway. This is a safety measure. If the pilot is unable to make a trap with his tailhook, the plane must have enough power to take off again immediately. Without full throttle, it does not generate enough lift to gain altitude. Without lift, the plane crashes into the ocean at the end of the runway.

Mark is intimately familiar with all the details of a carrier landing, of course, so he is well aware of the huge problems he now faces. With Keith unconscious, he needs to get the plane on the carrier. Now. There is no time to reposition the ship. But with a thirty-knot crosswind blowing, landing is going to be nearly impossible. And what if he misses the landing wires? He doesn't have nearly enough time to take off again and make a second attempt. Surely Keith will be dead within minutes.

Even if he can land, Mark knows there are even more problems. His mind racing, he begins to tick off other likely catastrophes. When the tailhook snatches that cable, the aircraft's forward momentum suddenly stops. But everything in the plane flies forward, just like the people in a car when you slam on the brakes. With Keith hanging out of the plane, and Lord knows what kind of attachment to his seat, there is a real danger that he will simply shoot forward out of the aircraft and be smashed to pieces on the deck—or perhaps gouged to death by the razor-sharp pieces of the broken Plexiglas canopy. But what Mark does not realize is perhaps the most frightening piece of bad luck of all: When Keith partially ejected, his parachute deployed. Now it is wrapped around the airplane's tail section. And Mark can't see it.

But, of course, what choice does he have? He must land the plane, and quickly.

"Mayday, Mayday," he says urgently into the radio. "This is 515. My BN has partially ejected. I need an emergency pull-forward."

"Roger, switch button six," comes the immediate reply from the control tower.

Quickly switching to the new frequency, Mark repeats his emergency request to the air officer on duty.

"Roger," says the air officer in a calm voice. "Bring it on."

Still more than six miles behind the ship, Mark knows he must get the plane on the deck quickly, but at the same time he is afraid of what any extra airspeed will do to Keith's already severely battered body. Quickly glancing behind him, he sees his BN, his arms blown out to his sides by the wind, as if he's been crucified. "He looked limp, and he was turning gray," Mark remembered later. "I thought that he was dead." Then suddenly he sees weak kicking once again, and he knows there is still time.

Deciding to reduce power even further, Mark slows to 160 knots, nearing the aircraft's 130-knot stall speed. While he is tempted to slow down even more, he is uncertain how Keith's precarious position might affect the aircraft's performance. What if the added drag created by Keith's body and the open cockpit makes the engines stall at a higher speed? Unwilling to risk a catastrophic stall, he maintains his 160-knot airspeed, hoping that Keith can hang on for a few more minutes.

But now he has another problem. His windscreen is fogging, reducing critical visibility. Turning his defog on max, Mark is about to unstrap his harness so he can wipe it by hand when the Plexiglas finally begins to clear. After what seems like an interminable minute, the pilot finally gets the carrier in his sights. And he is shocked by what he sees.

Instead of continuing in a straight line, the ship is in the process of making a long, time-wasting hard left turn, trying to move into the wind to make his landing easier—and safer. Frustrated and angry, Mark rolls the plane to the right to catch up to the ship's centerline, which he must maintain for his landing pattern. His tension eases as he sees the ship's wake begin to straighten: "Paddles" (the landing signal officer) has indicated that he is willing to risk the dangerous winds whipping across the deck of the ship.

This is it, Mark knows. He's going to get only one chance. At three hundred feet, the pilot is aware that the plane is descending slightly. This is wrong, he knows. Normally the plane should come straight in, then descend once it enters the glide path. But he is not willing to give the engines the additional power necessary to correct his position; he knows that every extra knot of airspeed lessens the chance that Keith will make it down alive. Mark decides almost immediately that he will go for a trap on the 1 wire, the wire nearest the dangerous stern edge of the flight deck. "I had no intention of passing up any perfectly good wires," he recalls.

Gently, he reduces power and begins the slow descent, almost gliding in. He feels the jostling thump as the plane's wheels slam against the deck of the enormous ship. For an instant, Mark panics. He does not feel the sharp, immediate tug of the wire. Did he make the trap? Pulling back on the stick, he hears Paddles yelling, "Attitude!" He needed to pull the nose of the plane up and force the tail down, reducing the likelihood of the tailhook skipping over a wire. His stomach turns over. He missed! He has to make another attempt! He's signed Keith's death warrant.

Then, just as he is about to pull the plane's nose gear off the run-way, he feels it, the reassuring slap against his seat harness. He's made the trap, caught a wire. They are down.

◉

Keith is in terrible shape, though he's still breathing. But the ship's doctor does not immediately run out to the plane. Because no one knows the condition of Keith's partially ejected seat, the first person at the aircraft is the seat technician, who makes sure there is no chance that any undetonated ejection charges will fire, sending the BN shooting off the carrier deck. Once the seat is secured, Keith is removed from the airplane and brought to the ship's hospital.

His condition is serious. His right shoulder, biceps, and forearm are paralyzed from a stretched nerve in his shoulder. His left shoulder shows signs of a bad dislocation, though it is not now dislocated. (Keith later speculates that it had dislocated from the wind pressure and then popped back into the socket upon landing.) His face is badly bruised, and his vision is blurred.

But he has survived.

◉

Why did Keith's ejection seat partially deploy? Upon inspection, it was determined that the ejection gun used to fire the seat out of the plane had been manufactured in the 1960s and had been subjected to years of stress from the G-forces created during flight. After this accident, the Navy removed and X-rayed scores of this seat model from other aircraft. Many were subsequently replaced, and a regular inspection program was instituted. "His harrowing experience [likely] saved another aviator from a similar, or worse, fate," said Aviation Structural Mechanic Paul Jung, the carrier's quality assurance representative for aircraft survival systems.

How was Mark Baden able to land the plane with Keith's deployed parachute wrapped around the tail section? In fact, the horizontal stabilizer on the tail is critical during landing procedures, and landing with a damaged or inoperable stabilizer is almost impossible. By some amazing piece of luck, the chute and its lines were wrapped around the stabilizer but did not impede its operation. "It was just luck, since it really should have done something. But the controls were not binding," Baden later says. "I didn't even notice that it was there."

In fact, not only did Keith's deployed parachute fail to interfere with the plane's controls but it actually saved his life upon trap, or landing. "The parachute became entangled in the horizontal stabilizer tight enough to act as a shoulder harness for the trap, but not tight enough to bind the flight controls," he later recalls. "If this had not happened, I would have been thrown into the smashed Plexiglas during the trap as my shoulder harness had been disconnected from the seat as the parachute deployed."

Keith slowly recovered from his injuries, and after five months had regained full use of his arm. Six months to the day after his partial ejection, he was back in the air. Mark was awarded an air medal for his outstanding performance, and the entire flight deck and tower crew were recognized for their successful handling of the mishap. In 1993, Keith left the Navy and took a job in telecommunications. Mark followed him in 1996, becoming a pilot for a commercial airline.

No one could have predicted Keith's bad luck, much less the series of subsequent events that saved his life. But Mark's knowledge of the plane, his familiarity with emergency and landing procedures, and his ability to translate this knowledge quickly into action made preparation an effective substitute for prediction. Defensive pessimism, it should be noted, is not the only effective preparation strategy for dealing with anxiety. However, in high-stress situations it can enable clear thinking by allowing the brain to rehearse multiple outcomes—especially negative outcomes—and plan for them accordingly.

Thanks to good training, quick reflexes, and some important preparation and planning techniques based on defensive pessimism, Keith and Mark are able to tell a tale of some very bad luck—but one with a very happy ending. "On my twenty-sixth birthday, I was blindsided by a piece of bad luck the size of Texas that should have killed me," Keith says. "Luckily, it was followed immediately by a whole slew of miracles that allowed me to be around for my twenty-seventh." He adds, "Murphy's law says whatever can go wrong will, and when you least expect it. Murphy was correct beyond his wildest dreams in my case. Fortunately for me, he failed to follow through."

CHAPTER 8

Parents Wait in Line for Hours

Al Kahn is jet-lagged, exhausted, and hungry, but he's reading comic books anyway.

On first glance Al does not appear to be the typical comic book reader. Middle-aged and close to three hundred pounds of mostly muscle, the former bartender and bouncer—known as Big Al by those close to him—looks more like an offensive lineman than a kid with a *Captain Marvel.* But when it comes to comic books, Al is a bit more discerning than your average reader, and he isn't out simply to kill an hour or blow his allowance. He is perusing not American comics but *manga,* the lengthy picture books read by millions of Japanese children—and adults. And he's looking for the next big thing.

It is early in 1996, and Kahn, a twenty-five-year veteran of the toy industry, is fresh off his eleven-hour flight to Tokyo from New York. He is making one of his frequent research trips to Japan, where he's been going since the 1970s, when he first saw a video game and subsequently brought Donkey Kong to U.S. shores, precipitating a toy revolution. On this trip, he's in search of interesting new entertainment concepts to license and bring back to the United States. With a stack of *manga* by his side, he's got plenty of potential candidates. The comics, more like the graphic novels found at home, can be hundreds of pages long, and a single issue may have scores of characters and dozens of episodic segments. Moreover, their target audiences range from children barely old enough to read to the elderly, and stories cover every imaginable topic, from schoolyard superheroes with mystical powers through changeling robots to hard-core pornography and fetishism, with everything in between.

Al is well aware that *manga* books as well as animé, their animated cartoon cousins, are gaining in popularity in the United States. *Dragon Ball Z,* an animé show syndicated two years before by the Cartoon Network, is growing in popularity, and older so-called Japanimation shows like *Astro Boy* and *Speed Racer* continue to draw cult followings. Other characters, including the Mighty Morphin Power Rangers and the superhit Tamagotchi, have also made inroads in the U.S. toy market. Al's goal is to convince the Japanese owners of many of the classic *manga* characters to sell him U.S. licensing rights, allowing his company to expose the cartoons to a wider audience.

Weary, his eyes bloodshot, but unable to sleep, Al puts down his comics and turns on the television in his hotel room. By chance, he sees a show, an animé, that catches his attention. It is the story of Ash Ketchum, a trainer of "Pocket Monsters," and the various battles that ensue among the many characters, including Pikachu, Cyndaquil, Chikorita, Kairyu, Yadoran, and Totodile.

The names may not mean anything to him, but Al knows that the Pocket Monsters are having huge success in Japan, having generated big sales of trading cards, video games, clothes, stickers, and other paraphernalia since their introduction a few months ago as a video game for Nintendo. He watches the show, not understanding the dialogue but fascinated by the powers of the animated monsters and the sheer number of characters—150! The merchandising possibilities are virtually endless. But could such a series be effectively translated for the finicky U.S. market? And would Nintendo agree to license the characters to an American company?

As he finally closes his eyes and begins to drift off, Al's mind goes back to 1983, the last time he can recall a kids' toy line that held such promise. That toy, a series of stuffed dolls, each with its own birth and adoption certificates and unique name, had been an international sensation, grossing more than $1 billion in sales. Al had been responsible for the national licensing of those dolls, and the phenomenon had made him something of a legend in the toy business.

Now, nearly thirteen years later, in a tiny hotel room in Tokyo, he knows he has seen the next big thing. And it is Pokémon.

❧

How do luck and business interact? Why does fortune smile on some business ventures and not on others? Why do some business executives seem to get lucky repeatedly, while others are dogged by series of failures? Does luck play a significant role in the success or failure of commercial products? What is this role, and how does understanding it contribute to our knowledge of the business of doing business?

It is often assumed that successful business relationships—those that create a profitable product or service—rely on a broad range of personal, social, and economic factors. These factors may include the number of previous successful interactions between partners; the network of other successful relationships that each business maintains; the professional and social relationships among participants; and the level of understanding and commitment in such relationships.

Recent research suggests, however, that only the level of relationship commitment significantly influences profitability in business partnerships. While other issues, such as relationship understanding and business networks, are important in building new alliances, both must work through relationship commitment in order to generate profitability for an alliance. And some researchers argue that profitable business alliances do not necessarily lead to commitment among participants. In fact, relationship commitment is influenced more by understanding than by profits achieved.

Such findings are consistent with the notion that, in business, the ability to recognize and profit from luck is based not simply on an individual's personal attributes but on a commitment to effective partnerships and strategic alliances with other capable players. In Al Kahn's case, this was particularly true, since studies also indicate that, in international business ventures, creating effective cooperative relationships and nurturing their development is critically important to success.

Timing, as always, plays an important role in business luck, especially in the fortuitous introduction of new products at socially and culturally opportune moments. But the recognition of particularly hospitable times for particular products may be less a matter of luck and more a result of the possession of a broad base of knowledge. Extending one's knowledge through reading, through personal and professional relationships, through travel, and through assimilation of a diverse range of information increases the chances that one will recognize luck when it appears.

Business relationships, information, travel, and timing are all key aspects of Al Kahn's amazing journey from working in a toy and hobby store to licensing two of the most popular toys in history.

❖

It is late in 1982, and Al Kahn, as is his habit, is making his way through a deep pile of newspapers and magazines. As senior vice president of marketing at Coleco Industries, he's constantly on the lookout for new toy ideas, or the sparks of those ideas, in the major media. Coleco, short for Connecticut Leather Company, had started out making leather change purses in the 1930s but had moved into aboveground swimming pools and then into the toy business in the mid-1970s, manufacturing kiddie pools, water slides, and plastic ride-ons.

In 1980 the company had had success with the electronic version of the game Perfection and its Head to Head series of handheld video games, taking some of the business of its archrival Mattel. In mid-1982 Coleco Vision, the company's console video game, had improved on the graphics of Atari, as well as those of Mattel's Intellivision, but it has now brought headaches. Warner Communications, the owner of Atari, has filed a $350 million lawsuit claiming patent infringement and unfair competition. Now, late in '82, Coleco is working on the development of Adam, a new computer for kids. But progress with that complex and expensive toy is slow, and the company needs something big for the Christmas season.

Al knows toys. His first job was as a buyer trainee at Allied Stores, a department store chain where he was put to work in the toy department. Because of his size, he could single-handedly unload the huge boxes of toys from the delivery trucks. He had gone on to import large arcade-style games from Japan, including Nintendo's popular Donkey Kong; it became the most popular arcade game in the world early in '82. But now, with video games being either imported or manufactured by scores of companies, Al knows that the intense competition is likely to lower margins for all involved. What the company needs is something different, perhaps something like a more traditional toy with a new twist.

He comes across a newspaper article that catches his eye. It seems that a sculptor and craftsman by the name of Xavier Roberts of Cleveland, Georgia, is doing a brisk business selling handmade dolls, often for significantly more than a hundred dollars each—sometimes hundreds more. The dolls, called Little People, are made from fabric and have pudgy, scrunched-up faces. No two are alike, and each one comes with an "adoption certificate" from "Babyland General Hospital" in Georgia. Roberts had recruited first his mother and then some friends to help make the dolls, and had eventually taken over a former doctor's clinic to create Babyland General, the place where the dolls are made. According to the article, since 1978 Roberts has sold more than 100,000 of the Little People dolls. And, Al reads, most of the people buying the dolls are adults, who view them as art, not as toys.

Al is intrigued, though he has a few reservations. The dolls in their current design are expensive, particularly for a toy that normally sells for far less than fifty dollars. And they are actually rather funny looking, not your typical smooth-faced, cute-and-cuddly squeeze toys. But he also knows that the idea of "adopting" the doll rather than purchasing it, and the unique identity of each doll, could really appeal to kids, who love the details and intricacies involved in collecting things. And, of course, kids want to feel special, even if they look different.

After making a few inquiries and determining that no one has licensed the Little People, Al flies to Georgia to meet Xavier Roberts and see the Little People in person.

◉

Xavier Roberts had always intended his creations to be individual works of art, not toys. Roberts had spent hours creating each doll by hand, and knew that they were relatively fragile. "I didn't want them to be toys," he once said. "Children are so spoiled, I was afraid they'd tear them up in two days. So I thought up the idea of the adoption certificate and the pledge they'd take care of the kid." But he also knew that once kids saw their parents with the dolls, they would want one too.

In 1978 Roberts and a few friends created Original Appalachian Artworks Inc. and began to market the dolls at trade and craft shows. With the help of an advertising firm, Roberts also began to introduce a detailed Little People back story and features that would appeal to children, including the conceit that the dolls were born in a cabbage patch, a story based on the southern folktale that all babies come from cabbage patches. He also began sending birthday cards to the dolls, a decision that helped make children feel more responsible for their "kids." And he had started to travel the country for doll-signing parties, spreading the Little People gospel wherever he went.

By early 1983, Roberts has found that his promotional efforts have paid off to such a degree that he can no longer keep up with demand. Since each doll has a unique combination of eye, hair, and skin color, and additional features like freckles and different types of cheeks, the labor involved in creating every doll (and making sure it is different from those that came before) is immense. With demand rising, prices have risen steadily as well, and some limited-edition dolls are selling for more than a thousand dollars. Finally, having sold more than a quarter million of his original handmade dolls, Roberts decides to license his creation, and let someone else do the work.

Roberts and Al Kahn negotiate a deal that enables Coleco to manufacture and sell an inexpensive version of the Little People dolls while still allowing Original Appalachian Artworks to make and distribute the handmade versions, which remain more expensive. Building on the folktale, the name for the dolls is changed to Cabbage Patch Kids, and by February, Coleco has them ready for the New York Toy Fair, the trade show where new toys are introduced to buyers. In fact, the company is new to all dolls, not just to this strange-looking creation. ("Coleco had never even made a doll before Cabbage Patch," Al later recalls.) But Coleco has found a way to machine-manufacture the dolls while maintaining each one's unique appearance and, while the Cabbage Patch Kids made by Coleco replace Roberts's fabric bodies with vinyl, they retail for a relatively inexpensive $19.95. At least, that's the suggested retail price.

By the middle of 1983, more than fifty other companies have been licensed to sell Cabbage Patch–related merchandise, including baby and children's clothes, bedding, rugs, cosmetics, a sticker book, card games, riding toys, and books and records. After visiting Xavier Roberts at Babyland General Hospital, Al is so taken with the Cabbage Patch Kids that he begins to carry around his own doll, taking it with him to meetings and dinner parties, and even giving the doll its own seat on the plane when he flies. "I never called it a doll, always a kid," Al recalls. "I always maintained the fantasy, the conceit that it was a real child, not a toy."

Al, Coleco, and the toy business in general are unprepared for the impact of the Cabbage Patch Kids on the industry. The dolls prove so popular that by the fall Coleco is manufacturing 200,000 a week and still can't keep them in stock. Market watchers begin predicting that Coleco will sell 3 million Cabbage Patch Kids in 1983 alone, a record for the introductory year of any doll. Coleco even suspends advertising for the dolls until it can keep up with demand.

By December, the Cabbage Patch Kids have become a phenomenon unlike any that's come before. Parents wait in line for hours to get them. Some stores begin to buy dolls for forty dollars (twice the retail price) and then resell them. At one store in West Virginia, a near-riot breaks out when 5,000 adults scramble to gain access to 120 Cabbage Patch Kids. "They knocked over tables, fighting with each other. There were people in midair. It got ugly," one store manager marvels. In Pennsylvania a woman suffers a broken leg after 1,000 parents, many of whom have been waiting in line for eight hours, rush into a store that has a small allocation of the dolls. "There's never been a toy like this," one store manager says. "When the dolls first came in, I thought, Who would buy them, they're so ugly?"

Who was buying the Cabbage Patch Kids, and why? Even today, toy industry experts have difficulty predicting the sales of a particular toy. Toys that test especially well with children are not guaranteed to sell, and successful toys like Cabbage Patch that depart from other popular toys of the time are particularly difficult to explain. But there are some theories.

"Cabbage Patch swept the nation and became the biggest selling toy ever," recalls Sean McGowan of PlayDate Inc., a toy industry research firm, "and much of its success was in the luck of its timing. Cabbage Patch could not have succeeded twenty years before 1983, and would not have succeeded twenty years later."

What was it about that time that made the Cabbage Patch Kids so successful? No one knows for sure, but there are some compelling theories. From 1976 to 1985, divorce rates in the United States were at their highest point in history, with an average of about five divorces per thousand people, almost double what they had been ten years before. With the rise of single-parent and stepparent homes, McGowan contends, the market was ripe for an "adoptable baby," a toy that fit with children's own feelings of being "different but special." Additionally, in a market saturated with impersonal (and physically cold and unappealing) electronic games and gizmos, kids were anxious for a more tactile experience, something they could actually hold on to and care for in times of familial uncertainty.

"It's very difficult for most girls to feel they look like Barbie dolls," said Dr. Bruce Axelrod, a child psychologist, in 1983. "The Cabbage Patch Kids, on the other hand, are not so perfect, and not so attractive. This enables the average child to say, 'Hey, this could be me.' " Axelrod added that most six- to twelve-year-olds also fantasize that they were really adopted or were born to another set of parents and were mixed up in the hospital. "Psychologically, this is a sign that the child is beginning to separate from the family, a necessary part of growing up." Al later recalls, "You have to realize, also, that at the time adoption was not out in the open, it was not something that people discussed publicly." The Cabbage Patch Kids helped children—and adults—understand that adoption was something to be celebrated, not something to be hidden.

But the vast, and incredibly fast, success of Cabbage Patch far surpassed that of a toy which appealed solely to kids. "Coleco made hundreds of millions of dollars in the first year of Cabbage Patch alone," estimates McGowan, who remembers the dolls and their impact very well. Those kinds of numbers indicate that the dolls were being bought by adults for adults, and taking the place of non-toy purchases: "People were buying them as investments," McGowan says. There were other contributing factors as well. The difficulty in obtaining a Cabbage Patch Kid conferred immediate status on those who were able to get one, a not-insignificant benefit during the decade of conspicuous consumption. "It was like, 'I got a Cabbage Patch, I must know someone,' " McGowan contends.

But if obtaining a Cabbage Patch Kid was a sign of social standing and financial security in 1983, the fortunes of the company that made the dolls were less assured. Coleco would ride the Cabbage Patch wave for two years, and sales of the dolls would peak at a staggering $600 million in 1985. But in less than three years, the company would file for bankruptcy, and Al Kahn would return to his roots in the video game business, in search of another hit.

○

Like many companies that get lucky with a single product, Coleco found that making the money was much easier than managing it. As sales of Cabbage Patch surpassed $300 million in 1984, the company began to borrow heavily to fund expansion and new products. But while its dolls were selling out, Coleco's other toys were not faring as well. Adam, the company's foray into the home computer market, was expected to sell at a pricey seven hundred dollars. It would dog Coleco for years.

To capitalize on the sudden craze for home computers, Adam was rushed to market too quickly. As a result, it was plagued by poor quality and major shipping delays. Coleco suffered a major setback after the magazine *Consumer Reports* published a scathing review, indicating that its testers were unable to get any of four versions of Adam to work. Late in 1983 shareholders filed a lawsuit alleging that top Coleco officials illegally manipulated the company's share price by concealing problems with Adam. The company incurred huge losses trying to get the computer to work before abandoning it in 1985. And though Coleco had profitable licenses to make and sell other games, such as Scrabble, Parcheesi, and the hot-selling Trivial Pursuit, by 1985 sales of Cabbage Patch Kids accounted for 75 percent of the company's revenues.

The danger, of course, was that Coleco had misjudged the popularity and staying power of Cabbage Patch dolls, betting that sales would remain steady or climb for years rather than trail off abruptly. In this vein, by late 1986 the company had spent millions manufacturing, shipping, warehousing, and advertising the dolls, tying up its money in excess inventory to support projected demand. Of course, Coleco was not the first toy maker to anticipate demand incorrectly. But the signs that such a strategy could prove disastrous were plain to see, at least for anyone who was looking. Worlds of Wonder, the company that had sold tens of millions of units of its popular Teddy

Ruxpin and Lazer Tag toys, had done the same thing in 1985. It had filed for Chapter 11 protection in 1986.

Predictably, as the novelty wore off, late 1986 saw Cabbage Patch sales plummet by more that 50 percent from the previous year. Even with the drop, however, sales were a significant $250 million. But because of its debt load, losses from Adam, and promotional costs for the dolls, Coleco reported a loss of $111 million. The company's chief financial officer resigned in April, citing "bad chemistry," and by early 1987 Coleco's stock price had sunk from $21.50 per share in 1985 to $8.00.

As Coleco hurtles headlong toward disintegration, Al becomes angry at the company's fiscal irresponsibility. For what he terms "political reasons," in 1987 Al is fired by Coleco.

By 1988, the company owes creditors more than $320 million, Cabbage Patch Kids are yesterday's news, and Coleco has filed for bankruptcy under a cloud of financial mismanagement.

❋

But with his reputation intact, Al quickly bounces back. By 1989 he has become vice chairman of Leisure Concepts Inc. (LCI), a small toy licensing firm with a fraction of the revenues of Coleco. In one of his earliest successes at LCI, Al parlays his contacts in the Japanese video game industry into a lucrative master licensing deal for characters from the wildly popular Nintendo home video system.

Introduced the previous year to widespread acclaim from kids and reviewers, the technically sophisticated Nintendo game system has racked up nearly $2 billion in sales by early 1989. In charge of more than forty licensees, LCI oversees the sales of Nintendo-based products that include lunch boxes, notebooks, ceiling fans, even a breakfast cereal.

But in a precursor of things to come, Al and LCI are also in charge of licensing *The Super Mario Bros. Super Show!* a syndicated TV series that premieres in September. By the end of 1993, the company's revenues have jumped to more than $8 million (they were about $4 million in 1988).

Al buys out his partner at LCI, and in 1996 his company has secured the master license for world rights (exclusive of Japan) to all characters from Nintendo video game products. But it is in 1997 that Al will discover what will become the biggest toy craze the world has ever seen, far surpassing even the Cabbage Patch Kids.

❀

In 1993, a Washington State math professor named Richard Garfield came up with a new kind of game for kids. Called Magic: The Gathering, the game allowed two or more players using special playing cards to pit their wizards against one another, employing magic to cast spells and control their enemies. Each fantasy card—there were two thousand in all—had a unique drawing of a creature, place, or magic spell. Kids collected the cards to create an effective deck, then faced off in multiplayer games or tournaments. By 1996, Wizards of the Coast, the company Garfield founded to create the game, had sold more than 2 billion cards, which retailed for about nine dollars for a sixty-card starter pack. Rare cards, such as the Black Lotus, were often valued at more than two hundred dollars. Many kids kept their cards in plastic to protect them from damage.

Satoshi Tajiri, a Japanese video game developer, discovered Magic: The Gathering in the early 1990s. But though he liked the collecting and competitive aspects of the game, he found a shortcoming: Because of its technical complexity, Magic: The Gathering was aimed at the

Dungeons & Dragons crowd, or young adults in their teens and early twenties. (In fact, the two games were such a good fit that, in 1997, Wizards of the Coast would buy TSR, creator of D & D.) But the thirty-one-year-old Tajiri, whose company was funded by Nintendo, thought there might be a market for a game with a simpler story line, using monsters instead of wizards.

"When I was a kid, I was very fond of running around fields and collecting insects and small reptiles," Tajiri said in 1997. "And I liked to watch *Ultraman* on TV, which featured unique monsters every week. I compiled all of my childhood memories into Pocket Monsters. Tajiri began to program the code for the Pocket Monsters video game, which would be released in Japan for Nintendo's popular handheld, Game Boy, in 1996. By early 1997, 3 million copies of the game had sold in Japan. A trading card game based on Pocket Monsters sold 2.3 million copies in six months.

In 1996, after visiting Japan and seeing the overwhelming popularity of Pocket Monsters, Al knows he has seen the game's future, and it is in the United States. "These things were everywhere over there, you couldn't get away from them," Al says later. But the Nintendo executives are skeptical. "Pocket Monsters was an RPG [role-playing game] that required a lot of reading," Al later recalls. "The Japanese were reluctant to license it to the U.S. because they didn't think American kids read the way Japanese kids do."

But having seen the popularity of Japanese cartoon characters based on the *manga,* Al feels the cute monsters with their various spells and powers might be a good fit. "We are always interested in licensing toys that help play patterns," Al says later. "Kids love to collect things, and they like fantasy games that allow them to control the universe." Pocket Monsters offers all of these attributes, and more.

"Kids really like to control things, and the power to control these monsters was really appealing," agrees PlayDate Inc.'s Sean Mc-Gowan. "But they also love to learn the intricacies of collecting, the statistics and the back story."

Taking advantage of the relationships he had developed several years before, Al is able to convince the Nintendo executives to allow LCI to serve as the company's agent, giving LCI the power to assign (and benefit from) licensing rights for all non–video game merchandise based on Pokémon, as the Pocket Monsters are commonly known, on "very favorable terms." "I had a very, very close relationship with the Nintendo executives," Al says later. "They were skeptical that the concept could work in the U.S., but I saw how huge it was in Japan, and I knew it could work."

Al's company introduces the tag line "Gotta catch 'em all!" to enhance the collectibility of the various Pokémon characters. In September 1998, following a multimillion-dollar advertising and direct mail blitz, Nintendo of America launches Pokémon in the United States, first with a five-day-a-week TV show, then, three weeks later, with the Pokémon game for Game Boy.

The Pokémon TV show becomes the highest rated kids show in syndication, even beating the *Today* show in the overall ratings on occasion. The Pokémon video game for Game Boy sells 200,000 copies in its first month. By October, LCI has lined up fourteen licensees, including home video, party products and stickers, electronic toys, and clothing. The license to manufacture a card game based on Pokémon goes to Wizards of the Coast (later bought by Hasbro for $325 million). By December, six hundred products featuring the Pokémon name or characters are available.

The Pokémon tsunami has begun.

❖

Though there are no firm numbers, experts estimate that sales of the Cabbage Patch Kids and related merchandise grossed $2 billion in the three-year period from 1983 to 1986, orders of magnitude more than any toy that had come before.

By November 1999, little more than a year after Pokémon's introduction to the U.S. toy market, Nintendo has sold 7 million video games; the top five selling games are the five Pokémon games released to date. Wizards of the Coast has sold more than 2 million ten-dollar starter sets of the Pokémon cards, and kids (and opportunistic adults) are selling hard-to-find cards on the Internet for four hundred dollars or more. When a Los Angeles radio station offers free tickets to *Pokémon the First Movie,* the switchboard reports getting seventy thousand calls *per minute.* Nintendo estimates U.S. sales for the year after the show was introduced at $1 billion. Worldwide sales by late 1999 have reached an astronomical $7 billion. LCI's earnings had been about $15 million in 1998, before Pokémon. For 1999 they are $60 million. The company's share price has gone from four dollars in November 1998 to fifty-three dollars a year later. In 2000, Al renames LCI 4Kids Entertainment, after his four children.

By mid-2001, Pokémon has grossed $15 billion outside of Asia.

❖

Why Pokémon? What made Nintendo's monsters the fastest-selling toy ever, bigger than Cabbage Patch, bigger than Transformers, bigger than Power Rangers and Teenage Mutant Ninja Turtles and G.I. Joe with the kung fu grip? Clearly, Pokémon offered a combination that proved irresistible to kids: Collectible items, a fantasy world of role playing, and the ability to control monsters were all critical to the toy's success. But Al Kahn, more than any other single person, was responsible for making Pokémon a worldwide sensation. How does he account for it?

"There's this misconception that American kids don't like things that don't look American," Al says. "In fact kids are always looking for something new, something different." While 4Kids does spend millions making sure that the story lines and other cultural cues of the *manga* and Japanimations translate effectively to American audiences, the look, the feel, and the basic premise of Pokémon did not change when it moved out of Asia. "As long as they understand what's going on, kids don't notice, or they don't care about the [cultural] difference," Al contends.

"The luck," he continues, "is in knowing where things come from, and being open to new ideas. You get lucky if you know where something might be, if you can identify it, and if you know what to do with it once you have it."

❁

In late 2001, 4Kids began preparing a new cartoon for kids' television. Called Yu-Gi-Oh! (pronounced you-ghee-oh), the story follows the adventures of Yugi, a geeky high school freshman picked on by older kids. By using an ancient puzzle, he morphs into a powerful superhero who uses clever games to defeat his enemies. The cartoon is slightly darker than Pokémon, but it isn't seeking the same audience. "We skewed it older," Al Kahn says. "It's really caught on among older boys because the monsters are a little more aggressive, a little more scary."

Since it began life in a *manga* in 1996, Yu-Gi-Oh!, like Pokémon before it, has been a hit for years. It has sold 23 million comics and 3.5 billion trading cards in Japan. But, some kids say, it's certainly not Pokémon.

"The only thing Yu-Gi-Oh! and Pokémon share," says one cynical seventeen-year-old who discovered the comics while living in Japan, "is the fact that Americans brought them over to make money."

Indeed, they did.

CHAPTER 9

As If Someone Has Swung a
Baseball Bat into His Spine

Steve Marshburn wants to cry out, wants to scream at the top of his lungs. He needs to scream, needs to beg someone to help him, wants them all to know, to somehow help him stop the excruciating pain, the pain that tells him his legs are being ripped off, the white-hot, searing flash of pain in his head, the indescribable pain in his spinal column.

Except he can't speak. And he can't move. He can see, though: People are all around, the crowds of people in the bank, all the military personnel from the bases nearby, all waiting to cash their paychecks. And he can hear: the voices of the worried bank employees around him, all knowing that something has happened, though not what.

But he can't respond. He is slumped forward at the teller window, where, an instant before, he was helping a customer with a transaction. Now he can feel the metal stamp in his right hand. It is burning hot. And, oddly, all the metal tacks in his shoes have suddenly come loose.

❖

According to the National Oceanic and Atmospheric Administration (NOAA), after floods, lightning has been the largest storm killer in the United States for the past forty years. While we often hear about people being struck by lightning, it is not necessarily a killer. In fact, most lightning strike victims (about 90 percent, according to NOAA research) survive. Most survivors, however, never fully recover, and many are left with severe physical, psychological, and cognitive problems for the rest of their lives. Steve Marshburn is one such survivor, and his list of medical problems is testament to the dangers of being struck. And, of course, being struck made him "unlucky" in our traditional understanding of the word.

But curiously, his story is not one of despair but rather one of hope, and therefore is illustrative of a key concept in any discussion of luck: the importance of using bad luck as a creative force for helping others. Steve's experience also gives us a corollary, which is that optimism—when applied to seemingly tragic, random events—can help us make sense of senseless acts, and help others prepare for them. As Steve Marshburn says, "You have to go through the valley to reach the mountaintop."

❖

It's a bright, sunny Friday in November 1969. The year that included humankind's first steps on the moon—and a little gathering at Max Yasgur's farm—would drop the curtain on the sixties and usher in a darker decade of military defeat and political betrayal. The country is in the throes of the war in Vietnam, with nearly a half million troops in-country. The Kent State killings are still six months away, but protests and peace rallies are widespread. Later in the month, on November 16, 250,000 people will march on Washington, D.C., to protest the nation's involvement in Southeast Asia, marking the largest antiwar rally of the era. Already, smaller protests and demonstrations are cleaving the nation, although the turmoil plaguing the country's big cities seems a million miles—and a million years—away from conservative Swansboro, in coastal North Carolina.

There are no protests in Swansboro, no antiwar marches. There are no peace rallies, no student sit-ins, and certainly no riots in this quiet southern hamlet. The war is touching the town in a different way, though. Just a few miles away, tens of thousands of military personnel are working and training at Bogue Field, a landing strip for Marine aircraft; the Naval Aviation Depot at Cherry Point; and Camp Lejeune, where the Marine Corps's Expeditionary Forces in Readiness are located. Today is military and civil service payday, and in this time before direct deposit, payday means long lines and a very busy day at the town's bank, where Steve Marshburn works as a teller.

At age twenty-five, Marshburn feels a fortunate man. An active churchgoer, he had prayed daily for a good wife and hoped that he would not have to spend fruitless, frustrating years on the dating scene. One day, while on the beach for a chaperoned church outing, he spotted Joyce and was instantly smitten: Her almond-shaped eyes, prominent cheekbones, and ready smile drew him in, and they soon began dating each other exclusively. Marriage followed shortly after.

Steve, their first child, is now three and, though he was diagnosed with cystic fibrosis, the couple feels lucky to have him and their coming baby, due in December. While he grew up dirt poor, Steve is determined to work hard for his family, and he's happy to have the job at the bank, where, with his southern charm and outgoing personality, he is a popular employee. He also enjoys the public relations aspect of the job, chatting with townsfolk and old-timers about the latest fishing exploit or the newest member of a family.

As he wanders into the teller cage, ready to begin work, Steve sees the huge crowds. Soon the head teller instructs him to open another window, and he notices immediately that there is only one closed window, and it's "the one," the spot all the tellers hate. The window is noisy: It is closest to the drive-through teller booth and the night depository. Reluctantly, he opens the window and, as usual, takes his place on a metal stool at this end of the long bank counter. He is vaguely aware that the drive-through teller, off to his right, has just gotten up from her seat; he guesses the line of cars waiting to make drive-through transactions has ebbed, at least for the moment. The teller's microphone, which is attached to a metal swivel arm, has been moved off to the side, making it easier for her to get back into her chair when she returns. Steve sees the sun streaming in the thick, reinforced window in the booth, which—because the ground outside is slightly raised—sits several feet higher than the floor of the bank. He pushes his black-frame glasses back on his nose, smiles, and begins to help customers.

○

Twelve miles up the coast, in Bogue, the weather has suddenly and violently changed for the worse. A storm has blown in—seemingly out of nowhere, since the day's forecast was for clear skies. Along with heavy downpours and strong gusts, there is a palpable feeling of static in the air. This area of coastal North Carolina is no stranger to violent, deadly thunderstorms: It's sometimes called the "lightning belt." The coast is particularly susceptible to the atmospheric instability caused by warm, humid breezes from the sea slamming into cooler air masses coming from the north and west. While they are now out of the especially dangerous summer storm season, Swansboro residents know that deadly storms can form quickly, and with them gale force winds, golf-ball-size hail, and, of course, lightning.

Like most lifelong residents of the area, Steve is well acquainted with the dangers of these storms and knows to respect their power. When he was a child and there were storms, his mother would make him and his brother sit at her feet in the middle of the living room of their small house, staying quiet and away from any metal in the house—including the screen door. The boys would listen, in both fear and awe, as the rolling booms of thunder and the sharp *craaaackkkk* of electricity filled the air. Sometimes Steve would think about his cousin, killed instantly several years before when he was struck by lightning while clamming at Sneads Ferry along the New River. Two other cousins had also been struck, one while serving as a lifeguard and another while installing an antenna. Years later, his wife's cousin would be killed instantly when lightning struck his home, traveled through the telephone line, into the receiver he was holding, and then into his brain.

Today, however, Swansboro itself is calm, and Steve is just hoping that the weather stays comfortable for a few more days. He glances over to the empty drive-through teller window, then back to the lines of customers talking excitedly about weekend leaves and plans for the days ahead. A few miles away, and several miles above the bank building, an enormous, deadly electrical charge is building. While the skies directly over Swansboro are clear, the trailing edge of the storm is packing incredible force. Suddenly, a bolt of lightning fires away from the storm and out of the atmosphere toward the ground.

In less than a millisecond, it strikes the metal and glass drive-through window, then flies through the underground speaker wire attached to the booth. From there, the electrical charge begins seeking ground. It races through the copper wire, up the metal swivel arm, and into the microphone. The microphone, however, is ungrounded. In a flash, the bolt fires out of the microphone, still seeking ground. Had the drive-through teller not gotten up, the lightning bolt would surely have entered her head and killed her instantly. Instead, it flashes through the air, on a direct course for Steve Marshburn.

❁

We often hear about the "tremendous odds" against being struck by lightning. In fact, while the odds against a person being struck are high, they are by no means beyond the realm of possibility (and they go down considerably based on geographic location). Ron Holle, a lightning expert formerly with NOAA, has calculated that, with a yearly average of 1,000 lightning strike victims and a U.S. population of about 280 million, the chance for any individual being struck in a year is about 1 in 280,000. While this sounds like a high ratio, in fact you are hundreds of times more likely to be struck by lightning than you are to, say, win the big Powerball lottery, where the odds may be 70 million to 1. And you are almost twice as likely to be struck by lightning as you are to die in a tornado (1 in 450,000). Holle has

also determined that your chance of actually being affected by someone struck by lightning (such as a friend or family member) is just
1 in 300, a fairly good likelihood. It is interesting that four out of five
lightning strike victims are male, although this is the result not of any
physical differences between genders but rather because men perform a greater proportion of outdoor jobs and activities. And while
we are often told to get indoors when a thunderstorm approaches,
as Steve Marshburn discovered, no place is safe when lightning is in
the air.

❀

The pain hits Steve like a locomotive. As he slams forward on his
stool, he feels an excruciating ache on the left side of his head, almost
as if someone is pulling his skull apart. The lightning has entered his
body at his lower back, which was parallel with the drive-through
window's microphone. Immediately, Steve knows he has been struck.
He feels extreme, unbearable pain in his vertebrae, groin, and legs, as
well as his right hand, where the charge finally exits. Unable to speak
for more than five minutes, he is simply an observer: Bank employees
and customers gather around to see if he is okay. It's as if he's in a
dream, or floating above his body, looking down as people ask him
questions to which he cannot respond. He wonders about the line of
people stretching out the door of the bank: Were any of them struck?
Shouldn't someone from the bank tell them to get inside, away from
danger? And why isn't someone calling an ambulance?

When he finally regains his voice, Steve knows something is seriously wrong. It feels as if someone has swung a baseball bat into his
spine. He has trouble remembering things people just said. His balance is off. His gait, once steady, is wobbly. And the intense pain does

not subside. Amazingly, no one at the bank calls a doctor. To others, Steve appears to be okay: He is not unconscious, he is not noticeably burned or bruised, and he is able to speak. No one has called for help, and most of the bank workers have returned to their desks. Afraid to leave his position at the window, he goes back to work.

Why doesn't he go immediately and seek medical attention? Because he knows if he leaves in the middle of his shift, he will lose his job. "I just had to work," he recalls. "I grew up so poor, I knew that I could not do anything that would jeopardize my job. I had a wife, one child with cystic fibrosis, and another child due the following month. If I was fired, who would care for them?" It is not until the following day, and at his wife's insistence, that he visits the town's physician (a "one-horse doctor"), who has absolutely no interest in treating any serious injury, much less a condition about which there was virtually no medical literature at that time. "This guy was only interested in head colds," Marshburn says, "and had no time for someone in my condition."

Indeed, his condition is deteriorating quickly. His vision dims suddenly, then returns. He experiences sudden hearing loss. His equilibrium is off. He can't sleep. His back locks up, making it impossible to walk. He experiences both short- and long-term memory loss. He loses his grip. He begins having bowel problems. He gets headaches so painful that they cause him to vomit repeatedly. He is bounced from one doctor to the next, eventually seeing more than a hundred in a fifteen-year period, paying out of his own pocket, since the bank refuses to file a report to the Occupational Safety and Health Administration, which might have made him eligible for workers' compensation. (Mary Ann Cooper, a physician and associate professor who studies lightning strike victims at the University of Illinois, says that

while up to a third of lightning strikes occur in the workplace, workers' compensation companies are often reluctant to acknowledge the
injury or pay medical expenses.)

What was Marshburn's reaction to his condition, and what does it
tell us about the effects of bad luck? Obviously, he was angry and frustrated that no one either could or would listen to him. No doubt part
of this reaction stems from the fact that in 1969 the medical record on
lightning strike victims was so sparse that his symptoms were difficult
for experts to pinpoint with certainty, much less treat. Another part,
no doubt, was his precarious financial situation: With no accident
compensation, he was barely able to pay his bills. He was also having
trouble concentrating and completing tasks, making work difficult.

With time, however, he came to the realization that, while unlucky, being struck "gave him a purpose," as he puts it. Indeed, replac-
ing anger with acceptance, understanding, and eventually, with hope
appears to be the healthiest course of action when one is beset by bad
luck. "When bad luck comes our way, there is no rational basis for resentment, since it only makes sense to feel victimized if what happens
is the product of someone's malignity," says the philosopher Nicholas
Rescher. People do not always act rationally, of course, particularly
when beset by seemingly irrational circumstances. But there is little to
be gained in being angry "at the gods" for bad luck and much to be
gained from adopting optimism as a strategic coping mechanism.

❂

Years pass, and Steve's condition seems only to get worse. His im-
mune system falters, causing him to fall ill constantly. He begins to
tire easily and gets confused often, finding it difficult to pay attention
when more than one person addresses him. He gets cataracts. He be-

comes disoriented in crowds. It's as if each piece of his body is breaking down independently. At one point, he has surgery for carpal tunnel syndrome caused, he believes, by electric shock damage to the nerves in his hand, in which he had been holding the metal teller's stamp. Steve's life has become a downward spiral, his physical condition deteriorating and, inevitably, his mental state following. Formerly easygoing and laid-back, he is now impatient and quick-tempered. He eventually becomes severely depressed, and ultimately suicidal.

Then, ever so slowly, he discovers a reason to go on. While watching television, he hears about someone struck by lightning. Reading the newspaper, he sees a story on an electric shock victim. Listening to the radio, he hears news reports on the dangers of lightning. He begins clipping articles. He jots down names when they are mentioned. In these days before computers, he uses the information-gathering and research skills honed at the bank to begin tracking down and contacting others who have suffered electric shock. He takes detailed notes, draws graphs, creates files, and, with Joyce's help, begins what will become, he believes, his life's mission: to help others who have been similarly unlucky.

Nearly fifteen years pass with little change in Steve's physical condition. While corresponding with other lightning strike and electric shock victims, he continues to work, to provide for his family. But he's becoming forgetful, and sitting for eight hours a day is excruciatingly painful. He hears snickers in the break room, fellow employees speculating that he's faking, making it all up. He's added fifty pounds to his once-lean frame. Life has become a string of doctors, each one less interested in his condition than the last, each new expert simply eager to write him a prescription and send him home.

Then one day Steve is referred to a new specialist. This time it's Dr. Rad Moeller, a rheumatologist in Pollocksville, about fifteen miles inland from Swansboro. He and Joyce reluctantly make the drive, expecting yet another brush-off from yet another doctor too busy to listen—or too tired to care. Steve reckons it will be his hundredth doctor in fifteen years. After describing some of his myriad symptoms, he waits for Moeller's response.

"Call his wife in," Moeller says. He then tells the couple that Steve is suffering from "lightning syndrome," a phrase neither Steve nor his wife has ever heard before. The doctor goes on to describe, in detail, other problems he is sure Steve is experiencing.

"It was as if God had opened a window to Heaven and heard our pleas," Steve remembers. "I wanted to run outside and shout, 'I am not crazy!' " Though he had not mentioned it earlier, the doctor had seen a number of other electric shock survivors and had been eagerly awaiting Steve's visit. It was as if the floodgates had opened. "I began telling him about the other victims, about all the information, the files, the charts I had gathered, the people I had talked to, and he encouraged me to continue," Steve says.

It was shortly thereafter that Steve realized he had a purpose in life, and that his bad luck, while terrible, had occurred for a reason. In 1989 he founded Lightning Strike & Electric Shock Victims International, a support group that helps victims of electric shock and their loved ones deal with the lifelong effects of these tragedies. With more than a thousand members in numerous countries, the group not only assists members but plays an important role in advancing the medical community's knowledge of severe electric shock and its effects on the body. And, perhaps just as important, it serves as a place of understanding, where victims can talk to others with similar ordeals. "We have saved many lives, talked many people out of taking their own lives," Steve says proudly. "And I believe—no, I know—that I was put here for a purpose."

❄

The power of bad luck is strong, strong enough to change the course of a life, even the course of many lives, from a single moment, a solitary event. Indeed, it sometimes seems as though people or families are cursed—the Kennedys are often mentioned in this context. Steve Marshburn's family has had their share of bad luck, too. Steve's brother and his family were killed in a plane crash. And his son-in-law was diagnosed with a brain tumor at age thirty-seven. If bad luck can be said to have a purpose, it might seem that its purpose is to vex our best efforts, to hurt us, even to destroy us.

But perhaps the lens through which we judge bad luck needs a wider view, and a sharper focus. Steve feels that every negative is simply a chance to create a positive, and in this way his bad luck was transformed into good luck for the hundreds of people he and his organization have helped, people who desperately needed assistance and had nowhere left to turn. "You learn from bad experiences," he says. "And one of the things you learn is that you either hate the world or you help the world. Being struck was my lot in life, but it happened for a reason."

Indeed, Steve's children share his belief that, rather than a curse, his bad luck was a blessing in disguise. "Dad's lightning strike seems to have been a blessing to our family," says his daughter, Stacey. "We have been able to reach more people by this act of God than we probably would have had the strike not happened. I think there is a reason for every season we have been through, and it is just building and shaping us for what lies ahead." Stacey's brother, Steve Jr., expresses similar sentiments. "There is always a reason why things happen," he says. "When I was eighteen months old, I came down with cystic fibrosis; I was not supposed to live past the age of six. My family and I feel that God spared my life for a reason. I don't know why, but he did, and I hope someday I will know why." Steve adds that "the Marshburn family is a blessed family."

Clearly, the family's religious faith and their trust in God have given Steve admirable strength and an amazingly positive attitude in dealing with his bad luck. He is a strong believer in fate, and in miracles. Does his story demonstrate, then, that these are requirements for making the best of bad luck? The answer is yes—and no. Researchers have found that faith does indeed seem to play a critical, healing role in overcoming adverse life circumstances (including disease). Such faith, however, need not be a faith in God or in any codified religious strictures; it need be only an optimistic outlook that tells you that things will, eventually, get better.

"Feeling optimistic is a reflection of our belief in and experience of our own capacity for the self-regulation of emotional states, especially painful, negative ones," writes the psychiatrist and researcher Susan C. Vaughan. Vaughan feels it is critical to use optimism as a source of inner strength and control when the going gets rough and when things are at their worst. Steve combined his religious faith and his desire to help others to generate optimism, in order to find meaning in his tragedy, and to gain some measure of hope amid his despair. While this strategy worked for him, optimism comes in all shapes and sizes. What matters, in the end, is not faith in God specifically but a more general sense of faith that things will get better, and the ability to maintain a positive outlook and not succumb to the pessimism that bad luck can generate. Furthermore, while some levels of optimism seem to be genetic, optimism is not simply an innate personality trait or disposition: It can be learned.

If he could, would Steve do it all over again? If he could return to his metal stool at the bank counter, if he could sit at that fateful teller window as that bolt flashed down from the sky, would he? Would he go back and be struck again? Would he relive the agony, the frustration, the disruption to his life and his family? Thinking for a long moment, he answers softly. "I think I would. Just think of the positive outcome."

Conclusion

Late in the summer of 2002, I was wandering around the clubhouse of a professional baseball team, interviewing a few of the players. I had heard that professional athletes are highly superstitious about luck—baseball players particularly so—and I wanted to learn more. After chatting briefly with a young pitcher, I asked him to describe his views on luck. "Oh, I don't believe in luck," he replied forcefully. Then he thought for half a second and added, "I make my own luck."

I was tempted to ask him which of these statements he believed to be true, since they appeared contradictory to me: Either he believed in luck, or he didn't. How could he state that he did not believe in luck yet in the very next breath take responsibility for it? Though I didn't push him for a better explanation (it was almost game time), I kept his comments in the back of my mind during the research and writing of *As Luck Would Have It.* Despite what the pitcher said, I felt, intuitively, that luck exists. It's like capitalism: For better or worse, and whether you believe in it or not, luck is inescapable.

But the guy did have a point. Unknowingly, the ballplayer was echoing the Canadian novelist Robertson Davies, who once remarked that "what we call luck is the inner man externalized. We make things happen to us." Though this probably overstates the case, it's not wholly inaccurate. While we can't actually make our luck, we can influence its impact through our actions, and we can in some respects control its effects. Dealing with luck is less a matter of control than a process of good management.

What luck management techniques can we take from the stories in this book? Clearly, each good- or bad-luck event is different, and each has its own particular circumstances, its own cast of characters, and its own set of results. But no matter what the event, there are some general steps that can better ensure the results are ones we can live with.

First, when possible, be prepared. As Keith Gallagher's story of the partial airplane ejection shows, it is crucial to integrate information from previous events—particularly those that occurred under similar circumstances—with our own base of knowledge. Defensive pessimism is a good preparation strategy to harness and control anxiety, though it is by no means the only one available to us. Any preparation strategy that increases our knowledge of potential dangers can help us deal with bad luck. Luck, after all, is a factor only when events are unpredictable: The more knowledge we can apply, the better we are able to prepare for luck.

Second, keep an open mind. As Josh Smith's story of the dinosaur bone in the desert shows, good luck is much more likely to come our way if we keep our inquiries loosely constructed. Be open to new ideas, and don't be afraid to fail: When one door closes another may open. While focusing on a single goal or a specific task may help us concentrate, it can also limit our vision.

Third, stay informed. As both Josh Smith and the toy king Al Kahn discovered, good luck comes to those best able to recognize potentially important objects and ideas. Read, stay abreast of developments in your chosen field, and be ready to act when you see something that catches your eye. Al Kahn saw Cabbage Patch Kids and Pokémon, while Josh Smith saw a blackened dinosaur bone in the desert. But both men were able to capitalize on these finds because their knowledge of their chosen fields helped them to recognize and make sense of things that a less informed observer might have ignored.

The stories of both Josh and Al also point to a fourth aspect of effective luck management: Stay curious, and know where to look for new ideas. Al chose Japan, while Josh chose the Western Desert of Egypt. Widely different places, to be sure, but both choices made sense for the same reason: They had produced important new discoveries in the past (video games for Al, fossils for Josh), and were likely to do so again, for the right person with the right connections.

Such connections are a critical part of the fifth luck management technique: Maintain broad, diverse circles of personal and professional relationships. Al and Josh knew lots of people, and these people had connections to other people in other circles. It is often said that good luck means being in the right place at the right time. But, as Al Kahn once said to me, being in the right place means nothing unless you know what to do with what you find there. Like Al and Josh, Pet Rock creator Gary Dahl and musicians Tommy Heath and Jim Keller had wide-ranging relationships with people who ultimately helped them succeed. Such associations may be lifelong, or they may be fluid and ever-changing. But they present important opportunities to capitalize on luck that are not available to those without such diverse groups of people at their disposal. Gary's story also shows that a belief in good luck may even improve our performance, and our chances of benefiting from it in the future. In short, believe in luck. Don't count on it irrationally, of course, but don't discount it, either.

A sixth aspect of luck management is to trust your emotions and your instincts. As Amy Knowlton found out during her plane crash at sea, being prepared for bad luck, and having the ability to counteract it, is often a matter of good risk assessment. Don't take unnecessary chances. And if something feels wrong, avoid it or, as Amy did, prepare as best you can. After reading her chapter, one might wonder why she got on the plane at all. After all, she knew it had had previous mechanical failures, and she obviously was safety conscious. Wouldn't she have done better to avoid the flight, thus avoiding the bad luck of the crash? Perhaps. But her presence on the plane, along with her handheld radio, probably saved the lives of the others onboard. In fact, she did not consider avoiding the flight. She simply took necessary precautions, because she trusted her emotions.

The wonderfully lucky story of Steve Roberts's lottery win points to the seventh aspect of luck management: Share your good luck with others. Luck is contagious, we often hear. Intrinsically, it probably isn't. But our actions can help to spread the benefits of good luck to others. Steve spread his good luck by giving both his money and his time to his favorite charities, which in turn helped many other people. If we come across a piece of good fortune, be it a winning lottery ticket or anything else, we make the most of it by allowing others to benefit, because they can then share their good luck with someone else.

Another factor in luck management is self-reliance, as Bennet

Zelner's story of being lost in the wilderness nicely illustrates. Believing in yourself and your abilities, and your ability to control your fate, is a key aspect of effectively dealing with luck (both good and bad). Bennet used illusory control to keep his spirits up, to stay positive and focused, and, eventually, to put himself in position for rescue. But the point is not that his control was illusory but that he was able to use the feeling of being in control to avoid panic. By not panicking, he kept striving, and by striving, he stayed warm, and alive. When events are beyond our control, at those very times when luck becomes a determining factor in our lives, maintaining a positive mental attitude and believing in our own abilities can counteract bad luck and provide a path for good luck.

Keeping a positive mental attitude is, in some respects, the most important aspect of effective luck management. Unfortunately, like good luck, bad luck is universal. But its aftereffects are only as bad as we perceive them to be. Steve Marshburn was struck by lightning and as a result suffered untold physical and emotional anguish. But his optimism in the face of bad luck not only helped his recovery but paved the way for his founding of a support group that helped thousands of other people who encountered similar bad luck. The organization was not there for him. But he made sure it was there for others.

Optimism is a powerful force, and it can help us turn bad luck around, for ourselves and others. Luck is not about being deserving or undeserving; in fact it is the very antithesis of any rational connection between who we are or what we do and what happens to us. But maintaining a positive outlook on life, in the face of painful evidence that it isn't at all fair, is an important step in recovery from bad luck.

And what of the baseball pitcher? By following the luck management techniques outlined here, could that confident young ball-player actually "make his own luck"? If the stories in the book show us anything, it's that true luck itself cannot be made. But its effects can be made to work for us—or against us—based on the actions we take and the choices we make. Luck, forced on us by external circumstances beyond our control, is one of the most basic aspects of our lives. It may be good or bad, fair or unfair, clearly deserved or without justification, but it cannot be eliminated. And elimination is not and should not be the goal. Rather, a better understanding of how luck can be managed is essential for anyone who seeks a lifetime of rewarding opportunities and endless possibilities.

Acknowledgments

Writing may often be a solitary profession, but no book is created alone, and this one is no exception. I was lucky enough to have dozens of people lend their time and expertise to a rather wide-ranging subject. *As Luck Would Have It* could not and would not have been written without the creative input and continual encouragement of my friend and agent, David Hale Smith. Thanks also to Bruce Tracy, Katie Zug, and everyone at Villard for their unwavering support for the book, from concept to completion.

Naturally, I am in the debt of those whose stories created the narratives that make up the book, and I wish eternal good luck and great karma to Gary Dahl, Keith Gallagher and Mark Baden, Tommy "Tutone" Heath and Jim Keller, Al Kahn, Amy Knowlton, Steve Marshburn, Sr., Steve Roberts, Josh Smith and Matt Lamanna, and Bennet Zelner. Thank you all for lending countless hours of your time, for recalling sometimes difficult memories, and for dealing with my constant stream of I-swear-this-really-is-the-last-one follow-up questions.

Thanks also to the following people and groups for their research assistance: Harriet Joseph; Jason and Tracy Franks; the Georgia Historical Society; the U.S. Coast Guard; the Philadelphia Phillies; Lieutenant Chal DeCecco; Jerry Burleson; Kevin Mackenzie, Bill Crews, and Terry O'Reilly for their Skymaster and aviation expertise; Stephen "Spaz" Schnee and Mike Paulsen for help with New Wave and power-pop music; Sean McGowan; Ellen Langer; Peter Darke; Julie Norem; Mary Ann Cooper and Ron Holle for their lightning knowledge; Deborah Bennett and Cesar Silva for their help with randomness and chaos theory, respectively; Paul Cheslaw, Terry Powell, and Alan Hunter for help on the recording industry and MTV; and Stephanie Olson. Special thanks and a big bowl of good luck to David Borgenicht for his continuing support.

And of course, thanks to my wonderful editor-critic-cheerleader–sounding board and wife, Christine. You are my lucky star.

Finally, it goes without saying (though I'll say it anyway) that all errors herein are my own. But there shouldn't be too many, if I'm lucky. . . .

Notes

Introduction

xix   **"an act of God":** *Life,* March 27, 1950, p. 19, in Warren Weaver, *Lady Luck: The Theory of Probability* (New York: Dover, 1982), p. 280.

xix–   **"For want of a nail":** James Gleick, *Chaos* (New York: Penguin,
xx   1987), p. 23.

xx   **The verse nicely illustrates:** Ibid.

Chapter 1

5   **Two out of every three:** Leslie Haggin Geary, "Rags to Rags: Millionaires Who Go Bust," CNN/Money online, May 8, 2002, p. 1.

5   **And these symptoms can afflict:** "Sudden Wealth Syndrome," Money, Meaning & Choices Institute, at www.mmcinstitute.com/sws.html.

6   **The May 2000 Big Game jackpot:** Nicole M. Christian, "2 Winners Share the Biggest Lottery Jackpot in U.S. History," *New York Times,* May 11, 2000, p. A-25.

8–9　**33, 2, 1, 12, 37:** " 'First Time Lucky' Ticket Will Split $363 Million," *Toronto Star,* May 11, 2000.

12　**A recent survey by *Forbes*:** Phillip Inman, "Treat the Rich," *Guardian,* November 10, 2001.

12　**symptoms that can result:** Claire Gascoigne, "Affluenza: In Sickness and in Wealth," *Financial Times,* July 15–16, 2000.

13　**"A flood of economic power":** Mark Levy, quoted in Laura Fraser, "The Experience of Being Suddenly Rich," *Industry Standard,* December 6, 1999.

13　**fundamentally test the basis of relationships:** Neil Crawford, quoted in Gascoigne, "Affluenza."

15　**money and happiness are not intrinsically related:** P. Brickman, D. Coates, and R. Janoff-Bulman in Tim Kasser and Aaron Ahuvia, "Materialistic Values and Well-being in Business Students," *European Journal of Social Psychology* 32 (2002): 138.

15　**the successful pursuit of materialistic goals:** Ibid.

16　**most satisfying life experiences:** Michael S. James, "Can't Buy Happiness," February 11, 2001, ABCNEWS.com, available from abcnews. go.com/sections/living/DailyNews/happiness010211.html. The article discusses a study published in the *Journal of Personality and Social Psychology* 80, no. 2 (February 2001).

CHAPTER 2

22　**Counties like Mendocino and Humboldt:** Keith Schneider, "Above California Flood, Days of Alpine Ecstasy," *New York Times,* January 18, 1995, p. A-16.

23　**Mammoth Mountain, the largest ski resort:** Bob Lochner, "It's Early, but Slopes Belie It Across West," *Los Angeles Times,* November 30, 1994, p. C-8.

23　**One observer likened driving:** Schneider, "Above California Flood."

23　**On December 4, 1994, Alan Austin:** Yumi Wilson et al., "Missing Bay Skier Found in Sierra," *San Francisco Chronicle,* December 6, 1994, p. A-1.

24　**A virtually unprecedented fourteen feet:** Schneider, "Above California Flood."

27　**At 5:30 P.M. sixty rescuers:** "Lost Skier Found After Two Nights in

Sierra," *Los Angeles Times,* January 7, 1995, p. A-20; Chal DeCecco, interview with author (August 2002).

29　**He does not tell them:** Chal DeCecco, interview with author.

32　**advice from survival experts:** Joshua Piven and David Borgenicht, "How to Survive When Lost in the Mountains," in *The Worst-Case Scenario Survival Handbook* (San Francisco: Chronicle Books, 1999), p. 148.

32　**Bennet was showing many of the signs:** Julie Norem, *The Positive Power of Negative Thinking* (Cambridge: Basic Books, 2001), pp. 99–100. The lottery and dice examples are hers.

33　**It motivated him to action:** Ellen Langer, Ph.D., interview with author (August 2002). Langer makes the additional point that, while Bennet might have been found earlier had he not wandered, he could have also been killed in an avalanche where he sat. The key is that, without his knowing the consequences beforehand, it made just as much sense for him to keep moving as to stay still, especially since he had no survival knowledge. Illusory control also allowed him to consider multiple positive alternatives (encountering people, finding shelter, getting rescued) while he was moving; only one of these was an option had he stayed put.

33　**In fact, his rescuers were constantly amazed:** Chal DeCecco, interview with author.

38–　**The rescuers add some words:** Carl Nolte, "Lost Skier Found Safe in
39　Sierra," *San Francisco Chronicle,* January 7, 1995, p. A-1.

41　**Research on depression and control:** John Mirowsky and Catharine E. Ross, "Control or Defense? Depression and the Sense of Control over Good and Bad Outcomes," *Journal of Health and Social Behavior* 31, no. 1 (March 1990): 83.

41　**In research studies, the absence:** Ibid., p. 81.

CHAPTER 3

45　**"Your new rock":** *The care and training of your PET ROCK* (Rock Bottom Productions, 1975), item 1.

45　**"A rock that doesn't come":** Ibid., secs. 1, 2.

46　**One man in particular:** Joel Sayre, "From Gags to Riches," *Scribner's Commentator,* March 1941.

47 **Founded just after World War II:** Spencer Gifts history, available from www.spencergifts.com/service/corporate_info.asp.

51 **"Ideas and products":** Malcolm Gladwell, *The Tipping Point* (New York: Little, Brown, 2002), p. 7.

51 **Such people may have:** Ibid., p. 33.

52 **According to one reckoning:** Jane and Michael Stern, *Jane and Michael Stern's Encyclopedia of Pop Culture* (New York: HarperCollins, 1992).

52 **A recent study in the *Journal*:** Daniel J. Howard and Charles Gengler, "Emotional Contagion Effects on Product Attitudes," *Journal of Consumer Research* 28 (September 2001): 189.

52 **Such positive reinforcement:** Ibid., p. 195.

54 **Indeed, research indicates that a belief:** Peter R. Darke and Jonathan L. Freedman, "The Belief in Good Luck Scale," *Journal of Research in Personality* 31 (1997): 506; Peter R. Darke, interview with author (July 2002).

54 **The precise mechanisms that cause:** Darke and Freedman, "Belief in Good Luck Scale," p. 507.

54 **"The superstitious feeling":** Nicholas Rescher, *Luck: The Brilliant Randomness of Everyday Life* (Pittsburgh: University of Pittsburgh Press, 1995), p. 175.

CHAPTER 4

58 **Recent research indicates:** Katherine Guiffre, "Sandpiles of Opportunity: Success in the Art World," *Social Forces* 77, no. 3 (March 1999): 830. Guiffre's article concentrates primarily on the visual arts, but she notes that her research is applicable to other organizations where networks of individuals are important to success. She references in particular a study of Hollywood composers by Robert Faulker titled *Music on Demand: Composers and Careers in the Hollywood Film Industry* (Transaction, 1983).

58 **This so-called weak-tie theory:** Mark S. Granovetter, "The Strength of Weak Ties," *American Journal of Sociology* 78, no. 6 (May 1973): 1377–78.

58 **Further, changes in personnel:** Giuffre, "Sandpiles of Opportunity," p. 817.

59 **The Fillmore Auditorium:** "Fillmore History," available from www.thefillmore.com/history.asp.

60 **"People were tired":** Stephen Schnee, interview with author (August 2002).

60 **"Nineteen seventy-eight was the year":** Mike Paulsen, "A Brief Overview and Reflections on New Wave," available from www.nwoutpost.com/nwhist.html. Paulsen runs New Wave Outpost.com and is an expert on the bands of this period.

61 **"The Knack was the first":** Stephen Schnee, interview with author (August 2002).

61 **An influential independent label:** Ibid. Schnee notes that Great Buildings was probably a bigger live draw locally than Tommy Tutone, at least until "Jenny" was released with the band's second album.

61 **But more to the point:** Mike Paulsen, "A Brief Overview and Reflections on New Wave."

61 **New Wave also had a distinct:** Paul D. Lopes, "Innovation and Diversity in the Popular Music Industry, 1969–1990," *American Sociological Review* 57 (February 1992): 65–66.

62 **In his early twenties:** Jim Keller, interview with author (September 2002); Mark Marymont, "Introduction to Tommy Tutone," in liner notes to *Tommy Tutone and Tommy Tutone–2* (Collectibles Records, 1997).

64 **Warner and its archrival Columbia:** Tommy Heath, interview with author (August 2002); Bonnie Raitt, in James Henke, "Bravo Bonnie: The Rolling Stone Interview," *Rolling Stone,* May 3, 1990; James Taylor and Paul Simon discographies.

65 **In a preview of the label's:** Don Snowden, "Bonnie Raitt: How Sweet It Is," *Rock Around the World,* no. 10 (April 1977).

66 **"I loved that tape":** Terry Powell, interview with author (August 2002).

66 **"I remember coming backstage":** Paul Cheslaw, e-mail interview with author (September 2002). All subsequent quotations attributed to Cheslaw are from this interview.

67 **In early 1979:** Tommy Heath, interview with author; Marymont, "Introduction."

68 **Scott had first seen Petty:** Tom Petty, in "Tom Petty: In His Own Words," available from www.superseventies.com/sstompetty.html.

69 **Columbia decides to release:** Marymont, "Introduction."

69 **In the spring of 1981:** "Nick History," available from www.nick.com/
    all_nick/everything_nick/history_home.html.

69 **Warner Amex, as the company was known:** Andrew Pollack, "Music
    on Cable TV Provoking a Debate," *New York Times,* November 29, 1982,
    p. D-1.

70 **It would be the first TV channel:** Marjorie Coeyman, "Cable TV
    Turns New Ground in the World of Commercials," *Christian Science
    Monitor,* April 16, 1981, p. 11.

70 **The goal, according to Robert McGroarty:** Philip H. Dougherty,
    "Advertising: Music Channel on Cable TV," *New York Times,* June 19,
    1981, p. D-15. The subscriber numbers are also his. It should be noted
    that, although MTV was the first all-music-video-oriented station with a
    national reach, some local cable systems had already begun airing the
    "promos" on shows for their local markets. Major acts at the time, in-
    cluding Olivia Newton-John, spent hundreds of thousands of dollars on
    promo videos, which occasionally aired on the big-three networks. A
    1981 ABC special featured Newton-John's videos, directed by Brian
    Grant, from her hit album *Physical.* Visit www.onlyolivia.com for more
    information. HBO's *Video Jukebox* also predated MTV by about a year,
    but of course HBO was not free, and still isn't.

71 **Because in the early 1980s:** Serge R. Denisoff, "Tarnished Gold: The
    Record Industry Revisited," quoted in Lopes, "Innovation and Diver-
    sity."

71 **Elvis Costello:** Lopes, "Innovation and Diversity," p. 66. His analysis is
    based on *Billboard* chart data.

71 **Micky Shine had also played:** Hugh McLean and Vernon Joynson, *An
    American Rock History: California the Golden State, 1963–1985* (Borderline
    Productions, 1997), excerpted in "Clover: The Story," available from
    www.clover-infopage.com/clpage03.htm.

74 **On August 1, 1981:** Peter Bowes, "MTV Celebrates Twenty Years," *BBC
    News,* August 1, 2001, available from news.bbc.co.uk/1/hi/entertainment/
    tv_and_radio/1465394.stm.

74 **"In the early 1980s, middle America":** Alan Hunter, interview with
    author (September 2002).

75 **"Once the people out there"**: Bowes, "MTV Celebrates Twenty Years."

76 **The album rides the song's coattails:** Marymont, "Introduction"; Tommy Heath, interview with author.

76 **"about 10 minutes"**: Tommy Heath, interview with author.

78 **"Everyone used to tell us"**: Tommy Heath, in Corey Du Browa, "Got Your Number," *Rolling Stone* News, available from www.rollingstone. com/news/newsarticle.asp?nid=5518.

78 **As one observer later noted:** Denisoff, quoted in Lopes, "Innovation and Diversity," p. 60.

78 **With the economy in recession:** Sally Bedell, "54 Years After Founding CBS, Paley Is Resigning," *New York Times,* September 9, 1982, p. A-1.

79 **In October, CBS closed:** Associated Press, "CBS Inc. Closes Plant in Indiana," *New York Times,* October 15, 1982, p. D-5.

79 **By the mid-1980s:** Russel Sanjek, *American Popular Music and Its Business: The First Four Hundred Years, Vol. 1, From 1900 to 1984,* quoted in Lopes, "Innovation and Diversity," p. 60.

79 **In the 1990s, the number of companies:** Lopes, "Innovation and Diversity," p. 60.

79 **In 1982, CBS and Sony:** UPI, "Sony Gets Green Light to Buy CBS Records," *Los Angeles Times,* December 23, 1987.

80 **Only in the mid-1980s:** Lopes, "Innovation and Diversity," p. 66.

80 **A *Billboard* survey:** Pollack, "Music on Cable TV." The quotations in the preceding paragraph are also from his article.

80 **Terry Powell later recalls:** Terry Powell, interview with author. The subsequent quotations are also from this interview.

80 **"Nothing could follow up"**: Chris Woodstra, *All Music Guide,* available from www.artistdirect.com/store/artist/album/0,,176105,00.html.

80 **By 1983, when 43 percent:** Lopes, "Innovation and Diversity," p. 66, from *Billboard* chart data.

82 **"We could no longer agree"**: Tommy Heath, quoted in Richard Martin, "Timbre," *Willamette Week,* September 17, 1997, available from www.wweek.com/html/timbre091797.html.

82 **one critic hailed:** Chris Woodstra, *All Music Guide* review, available

from   shopping.yahoo.com/shop?d=product&id=1921193051&clink=dmmu&subpage=desc#desc.

83   **"Yes, it's that Tommy Tutone":** Geoff Melton, *In Music We Trust Review,* no. 28 (February 2000), available from www.inmusicwetrust.com/articles/28r31.html.

84   **"I saw so many bands":** Quoted in Martin, "Timbre."

CHAPTER 5

86   **"The sagacious person":** Nicholas Rescher, *Luck: The Brilliant Randomness of Everyday Life* (Pittsburgh: University of Pittsburgh Press, 1995), 183–184.

87   **Of course, without good information:** Kristin Shrader-Frechette, "Risk Assessment and Uncertainty," *PSA: Proceedings of the Biennial Meeting of the Philosophy of Science Association,* no. 2 (1988): Symposia and Invited Papers, p. 511.

87   **when risks are shared:** Carol A. Heimer, "Social Structure, Psychology, and the Estimation of Risk," *Annual Review of Sociology* 14 (1988): 515.

87   **Behavioral evidence suggests:** George F. Loewenstein et al., "Risk as Feelings," *Psychological Bulletin* 127, no. 2 (March 2001): 267–286. The preceding quotation is also his.

90   **At the end of World War II:** Terry O'Reilly, Esq., e-mail interview with author (August 2002). O'Reilly is an attorney who has handled numerous cases involving mechanical failures with the Skymaster. The quotation is his.

90   **This and several additional fuel flow problems:** FAA Airworthiness Directives Amendment 39-1036 AD 70-15-02 and Amendment 39-5901 AD 79-10-14 R1.

90   **The plane has four fuel tanks:** Bill Crews, interview with author (August 2002). Crews is a pilot who sells Cessna Skymasters and has been flying these aircraft since the 1970s.

91   **Another odd aspect:** E. R. Martin, "Skymaster Fuel Management and Other Operating Tips," pp. 2–3, available from www.miramaryachtclub.com/337fuel.htm. The information in the preceding paragraph is also

from his article; Kevin Mackenzie, e-mail interview with author (August 2002). Mackenzie is the webmaster of 337skymaster.com and has been a Skymaster pilot for more than thirty years; Bill Crews, interview with author.

91 **Amy knew that their plane:** NTSB Incident Report, identification no. ATL87LA066; Amy Knowlton, interview with author (August 2002). The report states that the fuel-system selector valve had a known deficiency, and that lack of maintenance probably contributed to the initial (and likely subsequent) problem.

92 **Pilots of the Cessna Skymaster:** Kevin Mackenzie, e-mail interview with author.

94 **"Mayday, Mayday, eighteen east of Savannah":** Betty Darby, "4 Scientists, Pilot Saved After Crash," *Savannah Morning News,* January 27, 1987, p. 1-A.

96 **Based on Amy's call:** Ibid., p. 3-A.

97 **Savannah air traffic controllers:** William Clark, quoted in Darby, "4 Scientists, Pilot Saved," p. 3-A. William Clark was air traffic manager at Savannah International Airport at the time of the crash.

97 **Jerry Burleson, though he was monitoring:** U.S. Coast Guard Chief Petty Officer Jerry Burleson, interview with author (August 2002). Burleson says Masson indicated that they were "twenty-eight miles on the Savannah VORTAC, 180 degrees." It is unclear if this is what the pilot actually said or what Burleson heard, as the voice was difficult to make out. Though Burleson's recollection is that Masson said, "180 degrees," either this part of the tape was unintelligible or the pilot misread his instruments; a 180-degree radial from the VOR would have put them much closer to the coast. The plane was probably at the 130-degree radial, since it was found fourteen miles east of Tybee Island. The twenty-eight miles Masson indicated was correct. It's not clear why he said, "Eighteen east of Savannah" in his initial radio call.

102 **Masson indicates that he lost power:** Darby, "4 Scientists, Pilot Saved," p. 3-A.

102 **The fuel and valve systems:** Both Kevin Mackenzie and Bill Crews are

adamant on this point, and believe the crash was due to pilot error, although the FAA accident report does not make this conclusion. The quotation is Mackenzie's. The scenarios described are from discussions with both pilots.

103 **Another possible scenario:** Bill Crews, interview with author.

104 **But this outcome seems to be consistent:** Loewenstein et al., "Risk as Feelings."

CHAPTER 6

107 **Josh smiles to himself:** Josh Smith, interview with author (June 2002). Some of the details of Stromer's finds come from interviews with Smith. Others, where noted, come from William Nothdurft's book (written with Smith et al.) *The Lost Dinosaurs of Egypt* (New York: Random House, 2002) and John Prendergast's article, "Dinosaurs Lost and Found" (*Penn Gazette* 99, no. 6, July/August 2001: 24–32), as well as interviews with Matt Lamanna.

108 **Some researchers even argue:** Jerome G. Manis and Bernard N. Meltzer, "Chance in Human Affairs," *Sociological Theory* 12, no. 1 (March 1994): 54.

108 **"in the field of observation":** In Fran Slowiczek and Pamela M. Peters, "Discovery, Chance, and the Scientific Method," *Access Excellence Classic Collection,* available from AccessExcellence.org/AE/AEC/CC/chance.html, p. 1.

109 **"Much that is considered 'luck' ":** Thomas Pettigrew in Manis and Meltzer, "Chance in Human Affairs," p. 53.

109 **Thus, even in the seemingly organized:** Slowiczek and Peters, "Discovery, Chance, and the Scientific Method," p. 1.

109 **In November, Britain declared war:** "Egypt," Encyclopedia Britannica Online, available from www.eb.com.

114– **A new doctoral candidate:** Prendergast, "Dinosaurs Lost and Found."
15

117 **Forced to shut down:** Roger Highfield, "Meet *Tyrannosaurus rex*'s Big Brother," *Daily Telegraph,* June 1, 2002, p. 3.

118 **Then, in April 1944:** Nothdurft, *The Lost Dinosaurs of Egypt,* p. 19.

118 **In summer, cyclones blow:** "Egypt," Encyclopedia Britannica Online.

118 **Because of the ground's high iron content:** Nothdurft, *The Lost Dinosaurs of Egypt,* p. 97.

119 **"There were just piles":** John Noble Wilford, "Slumbering in the Egyptian Desert, a Titan of a Dinosaur," *New York Times,* June 1, 2001, p. A-6.

121 **Then, one night later:** Josh Smith, interview with author; Prendergast, "Dinosaurs Lost and Found."

123 **After running the numbers:** Josh Smith, interview with author; Highfield, "Meet *T-rex*'s Big Brother."

123 **The name means "tidal giant":** Matt Lamanna, interview with author (August 2002).

125 **"The mind must be prepared":** Lewis Thomas, quoted in Slowiczek and Peters, "Discovery, Chance, and the Scientific Method." The quotation in the following paragraph is also from their article.

CHAPTER 7

127 **The mathematician and author:** John Allen Paulos, *Innumeracy* (New York: Vintage, 1988), p. 33.

128 **While we may be able to predict:** Nicholas Rescher, *Luck: The Brilliant Randomness of Everyday Life* (Pittsburgh: University of Pittsburgh Press, 1995), p. 45.

129 **Just one day before:** Frank Beierly, aviation maintenance administration man, "Log of Activities of the USS *Abraham Lincoln* in 1991," available from www.gallagher.com/ejection_seat.

130 **As the plane taxis:** Lieutenant Mark Baden's account of the mishap, from www.gallagher.com/ejection_seat, and interview with author (August 2002).

131 **This strategy, called "defensive pessimism":** Julie Norem, *The Positive Power of Negative Thinking* (Cambridge: Basic Books, 2001), p. 5.

131 **"Anxiety is disruptive":** Julie Norem, interview with author (July 2002).

131 **Defensive pessimists, it should be noted:** Norem, *Positive Power,* pp. 43, 45, 125.

131　**Thus, while predicting bad luck:** Rescher, *Luck,* p. 175.

138　**"Mayday, Mayday":** Baden's account of the mishap, www.gallagher.com/ejection_seat, and interview with author.

139　**Instead of continuing in a straight line:** Mark Baden, interview with author.

139　**Normally the plane should come:** Ibid.

140　**Upon inspection:** Paul Jung, "Technical Aspects of Lt. Gallagher's Mishap," available from www.gallagher.com/ejection_seat.

141　**"If this had not happened":** Keith Gallagher's story about the incident from www.gallagher.com/ejection_seat, and from interviews with author.

142　**However, in high-stress situations:** Norem, *Positive Power,* p. 43.

CHAPTER 8

144　***Dragon Ball Z*:** Michael Mallory, "Kids' o7 Anime ff7 Hits Critical Mass," *Los Angeles Times,* "Calendar," October 12, 2001, p. 18.

144　**Other characters:** Joseph Pereira, "North America Braces for Attack of the Pokémon," *Ottawa Citizen,* May 27, 1998, p. F-5.

146　**Recent research suggests:** Desiree Blankenburg Holm, Kent Eriksson, and Jan Johanson, "Business Networks and Cooperation in International Business Relationships," *Journal of International Business Studies* 27, no. 5 (1996): 1046–47.

146　**Such findings are consistent:** Ibid., p. 1049.

147　**Extending one's knowledge:** Nicholas Rescher, *Luck: The Brilliant Randomness of Everyday Life* (Pittsburgh: University of Pittsburgh Press, 1995), p. 184. Rescher argues that expanding one's knowledge through the gathering of information can counteract bad luck where ignorance and not chance is the cause. And, of course, "one cannot win the race that one does not enter." I would argue that the same process vastly increases one's chances of capitalizing on good luck.

147　**Warner Communications:** "Coleco Industries Is Sued by Atari," *New York Times,* December 9, 1982, p. D-5.

148　**Because of his size:** Joyce Wadler, "He Who Has the Most Toys Never Says Die," *New York Times,* February 8, 2000, p. B-2.

148 **Roberts had recruited:** "Child's Play," Editorial, *New York Times,* September 27, 1981, sec. 4, p. 18.

149 **In 1978 Roberts:** Faye S. Joyce, "Fantasy Thrives in Birthplace of Cabbage Patch Kids," *New York Times,* December 4, 1983, p. A-30.

149 **With the help:** Sarah Booth Conroy, "Soft Dolls, Hard Cash: The Cabbage Patch Kids: A Georgian's Homemade Mania," *Washington Post,* November 30, 1983, p. B-1. The quotation is also from her article.

150 **Finally, having sold:** Ibid.

150 **By the middle of 1983:** Ibid.

151 **After visiting Xavier:** Wadler, "He Who Has the Most Toys," pp. B-2, A-1; Al Kahn, interview with author (September 2002).

151 **Coleco is manufacturing 200,000:** Philip H. Dougherty, "Behind the Cabbage Patch Kids," *New York Times,* December 1, 1983, p. D-23.

151 **Some stores begin to buy dolls:** David Bird, " 'Adoptable Dolls' Aren't Having Any Trouble Finding Homes," *New York Times,* November 29, 1983, p. A-17. The quotations and sales information are also from his article.

152 **"Cabbage Patch swept the nation":** Sean McGowan, interview with author (August 2002).

152 **From 1976 to 1985:** "Monthly Vital Statistics Report," vol. 43, no. 9(S) (March 22, 1995), Table 1: Divorces and Annulments and Rates: United States, 1940–1990, Centers for Disease Control and Prevention, available from http://www.cdc.gov/nchs/fastats/pdf/43-9s-t1.pdf.

152 **"It's very difficult for most girls":** Bird, "Adoptable Dolls," p. A-17. The subsequent quotations are also from his article.

154 **Coleco suffered a major setback:** "Coleco Stock Falls Following Report," *New York Times,* December 22, 1983, p. D-5.

154 **Late in 1983:** "Suit Alleges Manipulation of Coleco Stock," *Washington Post,* October 5, 1983, p. F-1.

154 **The company incurred huge losses:** Mark Clayton, "Coleco Misplayed Its Success," *Christian Science Monitor,* July 14, 1988, p. 19.

154 **Worlds of Wonder:** Ibid.

155 **Even with the drop:** Todd Beamon, "Coleco Sees Losses in Quarter

and '86," *New York Times,* January 9, 1987, p. D-3. The quotation in this paragraph is from Paul Taylor, "Coleco Officer to Quit," *Financial Times,* April 17, 1986, p. 27. The $320 million figure is from Clayton's article.

155 **In charge of more than forty licensees:** Michelle Healy, "Nintendo Hungry? Try the Cereal," *USA Today,* February 1, 1989, p. 1-D.

156 **By the end of 1993:** Figures cited are from LCI earnings statements.

156 **In 1993, a Washington State:** Laura Evenson, "Players of Fantasy Card Game Now Have Leagues to Test Their Skills," *San Francisco Chronicle,* August 6, 1996, p. E-1; Sean McGowan, interview with author.

156 **Satoshi Tajiri:** Sean McGowan, interview with author.

157 **"When I was a kid":** Sayuri Saito, "Video-Game Maker Scores Huge Hit with 'Pocket Monsters,' " *Daily Yomiuri,* June 26, 1997, p. 3.

158 **The Pokémon TV show:** Dustin Dinoff, "North American Pokémon Penetration Imminent," *Kidscreen,* January 1, 1999, p. 30.

159 **Though there are no firm numbers:** The figures cited are based on Coleco earnings statements, news reports, and estimates from Al Kahn and Sean McGowan.

159 **By November 1999:** Malcolm Jones et al., "Is Pokémon Evil?" *Newsweek,* November 15, 1999, p. 72.

160 **"We skewed it older":** Al Kahn, interview with author (August 2002), and quoted in Cesar G. Soriano, "Yu-Gi-Oh! Is for Older Kids Who Find Pokémon Passé," *USA Today,* August 31, 2001, p. 1-E.

161 **"The only thing Yu-Gi-Oh!":** Brendan Hubbs, quoted in Soriano, "Yu-Gi-Oh!"

CHAPTER 9

163 **According to the National:** National Oceanic and Atmospheric Administration, available from www.lightningsafety.noaa.gov/medical.htm.

165 **Soon the head teller instructs him:** Lightning Strike & Electric Shock Survivors International, Inc., *Life After Shock 2,* p. 1, and Steve Marshburn, interview with author (July 2002).

167 **Ron Holle, a lightning expert:** National Lightning Safety Institute, available from www.lightningsafety.com/nlsi_pls/probability.html.

167 **And you are almost twice as likely:** Statistics cited are from www.nhm.org/research/fishes/sharksff/sharkimg/sff38.html.

168 **It is interesting that four out of five:** Jacob Berkowitz, "Science Knows When Zeus Will Strike," *Ottawa Citizen,* July 11, 2002, p. A-5.

169 **Mary Ann Cooper, a physician:** University of Illinois, Champaign-Urbana, Lightning Injury Research, available from www.uic.edu/labs/lightninginjury/overview.htm.

170 **"When bad luck comes":** Nicholas Rescher, *Luck: The Brilliant Randomness of Everyday Life* (Pittsburgh: University of Pittsburgh Press, 1995), p. 143.

171 **He eventually becomes severely depressed:** *Life After Shock 2,* p. 4, and Steve Marshburn, interview with author.

174 **Researchers have found that faith:** Susan C. Vaughan, *Half Empty, Half Full: How to Take Control and Live Life as an Optimist* (New York: Harcourt, 2000), p. 9.

174 **"Feeling optimistic is a reflection":** Ibid., p. 34.

174 **Furthermore, while some levels:** Anne Bilodeau, "The Roots of Optimism," *Selfhelp,* June 21, 1998, available from www.shpm.com/articles/depress/deopti.html.

About the Author

JOSHUA PIVEN *is the coauthor of* The Worst-Case Scenario Survival Handbook *series. His books have been translated into more than two dozen languages and have appeared on bestseller lists around the world. He is a frequent guest on the* Today *show, NPR, and BBC radio. He is also a creator of the prime-time television series* Worst-Case Scenario. *He and his wife live in Philadelphia.*